BE A MOTIVATIONAL
LEADER
LASTING LEADERSHIP PRINCIPLES

LeRoy Eims

Run So That You May Win
ivictor.com

Victor is an imprint of
Cook Communications Ministries, Colorado Springs, Colorado 80918
Cook Communications, Paris, Ontario
Kingsway Communications, Eastbourne, England

BE A MOTIVATIONAL LEADER
© 1996, 1981 by LeRoy Eims

First Printing, 1981
Printed in the United States of America

23 24 25 26 27 28 29 30 Printing Year 07 06 05 04 03 02

Editor: Craig Bubeck, Sr. Editor over updating
Cover Design:
Interior Design:

Library of Congress Cataloging-in-Publication Data

Eims, LeRoy
Be a Motivational Leader/LeRoy Eims

    p. cm.
ISBN 1-56476-512-1

Library of Congress Catalog Card Number: 80-52904

CONTENTS

PREFACE

A few years ago I listened on TV to a widely respected Christian leader explain the function of leadership. He was talking to a very select group of leaders who were part of his denomination. He told them they should be like the animators who draw pictures at the Walt Disney Motion Picture Studios.

He told them that these animators are an unusual group of people. They can draw a picture of a mouse and by their skill as artists can make that mouse sing and dance and drive a boat and save Minnie from all kinds of perils.

They can do the same with a picture of an elephant. By their skill as animators, they can make that elephant fly through the forest, smell the flowers, and say hello to the birds and butterflies. And, "that," he told these leaders, "was their job." To inspire to action. To take something that is just sitting there and by the Word and Spirit of God bring it to life.

The dictionary gives this example: "The wind animated the flags." Can't you just see it? There droop the flags. And then the wind picks up and the flags begin to flutter and fly. And much of what God can use to inspire people to action is motivation. One of the prime jobs of the leader is to help people get fired up about the right stuff and keep them fired up.

And that's what this book is all about. I trust you will find it helpful in your walk with and service for the Lord.

FOREWORD

You're in for a treat!

If you are like me, you don't want an author to waste a lot of time and space getting to his point. Neither do you enjoy wading through pages filled with dreams, ideals, and theories that draw beautiful verbal pictures but lack the ring of reality. Especially when it comes to something as practical as leadership and motivation.

LeRoy Eims writes good stuff. If you haven't discovered that by now, you've obviously not read his other books. His world is the real world and his head is on straight. He faces issues directly, and he isn't afraid to come down on the scriptural side with force and confidence—another rare trait among authors, even Christian authors. But he doesn't bore you with the Bible, either. Where biblical principles fit, they are placed. But they are not forced. I especially appreciate that.

Although LeRoy has been engaged in various roles of leadership since his hitch in the Marine Corps in World War II, including his varied and lengthy involvement on The Navigators staff, I get the distinct impression he is still learning, still listening. He's tough, but he is teachable. Such balance is essential among those who are successful as leaders in today's world. His book will encourage you to develop that same balance in your own life.

You hardly need the reminder that we are living in difficult times. Threatening fears surround us. Instead of meeting the challenge of the 21st century head on, many people are running. Ours is a generation of "escape artists." We are desperately in need of relevant, reliable directives from the Scriptures that hold out hope to those who find themselves somewhat paralyzed by the sting of passivity. This book possesses those ingredients.

Like I say, you're in for a treat!

Charles R. Swindoll

CHAPTER ONE

Be a Responsible Leader

On April 25, 1980, when the fifty Americans had already been held hostage in Iran for 173 days, President Carter appeared on television. In a solemn voice, he disclosed to the American people that a United States military team had failed in its attempt to rescue the fifty Americans held hostage in the American Embassy in Teheran, Iran. After the President described the events that led to the aborted mission, he stated, "It was my decision to attempt the rescue operation. It was my decision to cancel it when problems developed. The responsibility is fully my own."

President Carter realized that where the interests of the United States are concerned, the buck stops at the President's desk.

Responsibility

Whatever the enterprise, the leader is responsible for the success or failure of the mission. But how hard it is for most leaders to accept the responsibility for what happens in their organization!

In the summer of 1979, the National Aeronautics and Space Administration had a problem. NASA was held responsible for something over which it had little control: Skylab was failing. NASA had built Skylab, bragged about it, and launched it, and now it was in trouble. Tons of metal that had been orbiting the earth would soon come tumbling down. But where? On somebody's head? On somebody's horse? On somebody's house? No one was quite sure. So the world and NASA waited.

To some, the idea of a hunk of metal, nine stories tall and weighing 77.5 tons, crashing to earth was greeted with humor and lighthearted jokes. Chicken Little was paraphrased: "The Skylab is falling! The Skylab is falling!" Parties were given to which guests wore feathers and chicken beaks. Some people wore T-shirts displaying a bull's-eye and the words, "I'm an official Skylab target."

But there was a serious side as well. Many people felt themselves at the mercy of a force over which nobody had control. Some were fearful. Some were angry. Others grew resentful because the people who were responsible had let the situation get out of hand. They complained that NASA should have thought about this eventuality and made proper plans to bring Skylab back safely.

NASA claimed that although there were some probabilities, they could not predict with any degree of accuracy where the thing would come down. Although NASA was responsible for placing Skylab in orbit, it did not accept responsibility for where it would land.

Motivation and Morale

Let's think for a moment how that event relates to motivation and morale. If a group gets the feeling that its leader is not doing his or her job—or is not taking full responsibility for what is happening in the enterprise—the members will often become resentful, cynical, or fearful. As they grow dissatisfied with their leadership, motivation and morale will plummet. An incident that occurred in an American corporation dramatically illustrates this truth. The administration was in the midst of a personnel problem of tremendous proportions, and the leader adamantly refused to be involved in the solution. By his actions he communicated to his top people that he felt no sense of responsibility for the cause of the problem, nor did he have any interest in leading them through it. The men and women closest to him became frustrated, angry, and despondent. Finally, they confronted the man and told him that because of his failure to lead, they were ready to quit. After a lengthy and heated discussion, the leader was jolted into the world of reality, and promised to do all within his power to resolve the situation. And when the leader accepted his responsibility, the people could unite with him and as a team begin to work together.

Although several factors affect motivation and morale, one of the key factors is responsible leadership. The leaders who take full responsibility for their own actions, and for the people over whom God has placed them, will command loyalty and respect.

The week after the United States' abortive attempt to rescue the hostages in Iran, I was speaking to a group of servicemen and women at a conference in Virginia. One of the officers told me of a speech given in the Pentagon by a high-ranking general. This general said that the sense of guilt he felt over the failure of the mission was more than offset by the sense of pride he felt toward his commander in chief for publicly taking full responsibility for the decisions that had been made. The officer who told me that story said that he and the rest of the men and women who served with him at the Pentagon were also greatly moved to rally behind the President. The fact that the President had accepted responsibility commanded their loyalty and respect.

Rationalization

But all too often the leader is tempted to pass the buck—to squirm out of taking the responsibility for something bad and unpleasant. We all have this tendency. It's part of our nature. For example, if I put on a few inches around my middle, I can easily blame my dad. I can rationalize, "He was a big, heavy man, and I take right after him. If I had had a skinny dad, things would be different. But because my dad was fat, I am doomed to put on weight. It's all his fault." I ignore the fact that I eat ice cream, popcorn, and chocolate-covered peanuts.

Somehow that's immaterial. I rationalize that I inherited my proneness to gain weight easily and so can place the blame squarely where it belongs—on my dad.

The Bible has something to say about this kind of phony rationalization. God holds people responsible for their actions. God holds a leader responsible for what takes place in the ranks. The leader is a prime means God uses to keep His people moving in the right direction and doing the right thing. The one who leads the band must face the music.

We can see a clear picture of this principle in the giving of manna to the Children of Israel. The Lord had been clear in His instructions. They were to gather manna six days of the week but not on the Sabbath. However, some disobeyed. "Some of the people went out on the seventh day to gather it, but they found none. Then the LORD said to Moses, 'How long will you refuse to keep my commands and my instruction?'" (Ex. 16:27-28).

Amazing! Had Moses broken the commandments and laws of God? No! Some of the people had, but not Moses. But look whom the Lord held responsible! The leader! God wanted Moses to be ever on the alert, so that the sins of the people would not be due to neglect or sloth on his part. He wanted the man whom He put in charge to be on top of the situation; for in the final analysis, Moses would be held responsible.

Overcoming Rationalization

Because of our natural tendency to rationalize, we need to recognize this weakness and then battle against it.

"Better a patient man than a warrior, a man who controls his temper than one who takes a city" (Prov. 16:32). It is better to conquer yourself than to conquer others. But conquering yourself is difficult, because you are dealing with your own corrupt, unruly, compromising spirit that so easily justifies its actions and tries to wriggle out of assuming the responsibility for them. Just as allowing yourself the luxury of losing your temper, wallowing in self-pity, or indulging your fleshly appetites is sin, so trying to shift the blame for your actions is also sin.

When you as the leader fail to deal with sin in your own life, the people who work with you will soon lose confidence in you. If you are the leader, you must arm yourself for a lifetime of fighting against your natural tendencies toward self-indulgence and your proneness to blame others when you should assume responsibility.

The heart is the field in which these battles are fought. And that is an unnerving thought. "The heart is deceitful above all things and beyond cure. Who can understand it?" (Jer. 17:9). One mighty truth surfaces in the context of this passage—I am a fool to depend on the strength of my own nature instead of depending on the wisdom and power of God. The heart, being sinister and deceptive, declares evil to be good and good to be evil. We all imagine our hearts to be better than they are. In fact, the human heart will allow us to vindicate ourselves in self-deception. The heart will be the ringleader to camouflage the path to ruin.

But if we turn to God and ask Him to cast light on our darkness and show us the truth, He will do it. David's prayer is our model. "Search me, O God, and know my heart; test me and know my anxious thoughts. See if there is any offensive way in me, and lead me in the way everlasting" (Ps. 139:23-24). God knows us. We flatter and justify ourselves, and march blindly toward the brink of disaster; but God in His mercy brings the light of truth to jolt us to our senses.

Accept Responsibility

The application is plain. Whenever I am tempted to succumb to the devious shenanigans of my deceitful heart, I can meet them head-on and triumph over them in the strength of the Lord. If I am responsible for something that goes awry, I must acknowledge my responsibility and set it right. This is not an easy thing to do. The "taking of the city" in physical conflict is child's play compared with the daily, unceasing conflict with my unknowable, deceitful heart. The U.S. Navy has a saying: "It didn't happen on my watch." It means, "I wasn't to blame. It was not my fault." But when God speaks to me and shows me my sin, I had better listen. My heart is always deceitful. God is always true. The choice is mine: I can follow truth or deceit.

If I ignore what God tells me, I am the one responsible, and I will suffer the consequences. "If you are wise, your wisdom will reward you; if you are a mocker, you alone will suffer" (Prov. 9:12). The aftermath of my actions comes back to roost on my own head. If I behave falsely toward myself or toward the people God has placed in my oversight, I wrong my own soul (Prov. 8:36). I cannot pass the buck to someone else to avoid my responsibility.

When God confronted Adam with his sin, Adam could have said,

"Yes, God, You're right." But he didn't. He tried to pass the buck to Eve, but it didn't work. Eve, in turn, tried to blame the serpent, but that didn't work. Trying to weasel out of responsibility is as old as the Garden of Eden.

But chickens do come home to roost. The evil results of poor performance eventually overtake us. The frightening thing is that these results may plague an enterprise for years, decades, even centuries! We are still smarting under the results of Adam's sin.

There are numerous areas where a leader needs to accept responsibility. Solomon addressed five important responsibilities that belong to the leader.

1. *Rebuke or correct.* Leaders must accept responsibility to rebuke sin in the ranks or to correct an improper course of action taken by someone under their charge. At times leaders see an improper course of action and refuse to correct it because they are afraid of losing the favor of the people. "He who rebukes a man will in the end gain more favor than he who has a flattering tongue" (Prov. 28:23).

2. *Act decisively.* When the opportunity arises to do something of noble worth and profound consequence, leaders must accept the responsibility to act decisively. Solomon said that if a person excuses unjust behavior by saying he didn't know about it, he would still answer to God who weighs the heart and repays every man according to his works.

To see a fellow human being in imminent danger, on the brink of disaster, and to do nothing is a crime in the sight of God and man. The people will look upon such leaders as heartless and uncaring or as cowards. However, if leaders spot a need, roll up their sleeves, step in, and do whatever they can, their followers will be motivated to join in as well.

When I was in a city in the American Southwest, I heard a man pouring out his heart for his fellowmen across the sea in Southeast Asia. These people were starving and being brutalized, but their borders were closed to any kind of humanitarian aid and relief. Moved by the need, this man got involved. He called representatives in the United Nations, the Red Cross, various ambassadors of nearby countries, Christian relief agencies, and so on. Everyone said the same thing. "There is nothing we can do. The oppressors are in control. They will allow no one to bring comfort and aid."

But John did not stop. He began to mobilize a great prayer effort among Christians. I listened to him in a home meeting. The next day his pastor permitted him to lay the burden before the congregation at the Sunday morning worship service. He was on the phone to friends across America and around the world. His plea was that people would pray.

Everyone who heard John was challenged and motivated. And many got behind him and helped him in his effort. He was a leader who commanded love and respect. He saw an opportunity to do something of noble worth and profound consequence and did it. He motivated thousands of people to pray that God might open ways to send relief to needy people.

3. *Listen to criticism.* Leaders should accept responsibility to listen to criticism from the ranks. "Whoever heeds correction shows prudence" (Prov. 15:5), but "He who hates correction will die" (Prov. 15:10). There is hope for people who take their medicine. But if people are sick, visit the doctor, get medicine, and then refuse to take it, they might as well have avoided the whole process. Solomon went on to say, "Listen to advice and accept instruction, and in the end you will be wise" (Prov. 19:20).

Throughout the Bible we see the value of an eager learner's spirit on the part of the leader. But all too often we see the picture of people closed to counsel and on their way to ruin. If we see this in a leader, we may desert him or her, and rightly so. God has not given us life to be spent heading in the wrong direction, doing the wrong things, under the leadership of a person who will not listen to wise, constructive criticism.

4. *Be honest.* Leaders should accept responsibility to keep everything open and above-board. Over the years on the international scene, we have seen giant corporations taken to task for bribery. We see the same problems on the national level, as the sins of leaders are exposed. Solomon spoke to this. "A fool's mouth is his undoing, and his lips are a snare to his soul" (Prov. 18:7). A leader should tell the truth. One of the

great kings of France is reported to have said, "If truth be banished from all the rest of the world, it ought to be found in the hearts of princes."

If leaders are not honest, their deception will soon be discovered; and the morale and motivation of the people will plummet.

No one likes to be led by a liar. The person in the ranks hates to be deceived. To be known as a member of a group being led by a liar is humiliating. The lies of the leader reflect on the integrity of every person on the team.

A leader is often tempted to lie to cover up a mistake or failure. However, to do so is madness, for the lie will eventually come to light. A leader's best course of action is to face up to the problem immediately, ask forgiveness of the people, and enlist their aid in setting things right. This is clear evidence that the leader is taking responsibility for his or her actions.

5. *Be fair.* Leaders should accept responsibility to deal fairly with their people. "The LORD abhors dishonest scales, but accurate weights are his delight" (Prov. 11:1). Apparently, there was a widespread custom of having different weights and means of measurement for buying and selling—one stone too heavy and another too light. To take advantage of the unsuspecting is an abomination to God and a crime against mankind.

A garage owner once told me of a lady who had brought her automobile to him for repairs. For many years she had relied on a certain automobile mechanic to keep her car in good running order. One day this man deliberately did something to the engine to make it run improperly. He then told her she needed major engine repairs. Through a series of circumstances, the lady discovered what he had done. She was angry that he had tried to cheat her out of her money, but more than that she was deeply hurt that the man whom she had trusted for years had attempted to deceive her. The confidence she had placed in him had been violated. She had trusted his judgment and had believed his word. And he had deliberately taken advantage of her trust to use it for his own gain. People rely on a leader in the same way as this woman had relied on the mechanic. And like this woman, when their confidence is betrayed, followers will often turn to another leader.

If any leader is to command a following, he or she must accept responsibility. That's one of the requirements of leadership. I was greatly challenged one day years ago by a sign on the wall of the Manila bus depot. It read, "The superintendent of the Manila bus depot is responsible for everything that does or does not happen in the Manila bus depot." Now that's what I call taking responsibility! How would you like to be held accountable for everything that *didn't* happen in the Manila bus depot! But I knew what he meant, and I agreed with him. Had I been able to find him, I would have shaken his hand and complimented him.

Leaders must make a choice. They can accept responsibility, as the Manila bus depot superintendent did, or they can pin the blame somewhere else.

What kind of leader are you? Are you armed to fight your natural tendency to justify yourself and blame others? Are you trusting God and His Word to help you overcome the deceitfulness of your own heart? Are you listening to what God tells you? God *does* hold His leaders responsible. If you want to lead the band, you have to face the music!

CHAPTER TWO

Be a Growing Leader

Leaders must be sure they are always growing. Continual growth is a key to effective leadership, and God is the key to growth. There are, however, certain things that leaders can do to activate the growth process.

One of the keys to leaders' growth is God's Word (Acts 20:32). But to grow by it, they must spend time in it. As Solomon said, "How much better to get wisdom than gold, to choose understanding rather than silver!" (Prov. 16:16) Notice that it is not just better, but *much* better. This is rather like trying to compare a drinking fountain with Victoria Falls. Or comparing the brilliance of a sunset with the striking of a match. But think for a moment—If you were to ask a group of Christians whether they would rather have the opportunity to spend an hour, either filling a basket with silver and gold or reading the Word of God, which do you think they would choose? In thousands of homes, the Book that contains the wisdom of God and proper understanding of life goes unopened.

Wouldn't it be exciting to see people whose hunger for the Word of God outweighed their craving for the treasures of the earth? Both are actually gifts from God, but the gift of God's grace and wisdom should be greatly preferred. Grace involves eternity. The treasures of earth are temporal. Thousands struggle and claw after the wealth of the world and never attain it. (See Prov. 23:4-5.) They spend their lives in frustration.

But the gift of grace and the wisdom of God are never denied. The man or woman who seeks shall find. To the one who knocks, it is opened. The one who asks will receive. Frustration gives way to satisfaction. The soul is at peace. The mind is enlightened, and the spirit motivated by heavenly truth. To trade all of that for Esau's mess of pottage is madness. Yet many do.

Leaders are tempted to give their lives to temporal things, and they need to be alert to the warnings of Jesus. "[What was sown] among the thorns is the man who hears the word, but the worries of this life and the deceitfulness of wealth choke it, making it unfruitful" (Matt. 13:22). The cares of this world can sap the leader's energy. The deceitfulness of riches and lust for glory can divert him or her. The desire for personal gain and power is there. And all too many succumb to its allurements.

Now and then we see the fall of Christians who were thought to be sturdy oaks in the kingdom of God. What is behind their failure? Many things, but one, for sure. At some point in their lives, they were diverted from those disciplines that encourage personal growth. And when this began to happen, the astute among their followers were devastated, their morale crushed and their motivation brought low.

On a plane trip once, I was discussing this with a young executive. He told me of the problems his company was facing. Products were being delayed in distribution. There was hostility among the employees, and some had resigned in anger. The business was a mess and the morale of the company was lower than a duck's instep. I asked the young executive what the real cause of the problem was and what he saw as a solution. His words were crisp and to the point. "Our problem is leadership. The man in charge has not grown with the job. When he came to work for us, all was well. He was competent in his job. Now, business has dramatically increased and production is way up. But the top man has remained stagnant. We've got to replace him."

To avoid this type of problem, leaders must continue to grow in both their personal and spiritual lives, and in their ability to perform their jobs. I remember being in a meeting with Dawson Trotman, founder of The Navigators, shortly before his death. He came bouncing into the room with a smile on his face and his eyes dancing. "Let me share a verse with you that God gave to me this morning in my quiet time. I don't know how I've lived all these years without this precious verse written on the table of my heart." I was greatly challenged. Here was our leader still setting the example in spiritual growth. Simple things like this motivate people and make for high morale.

Growth is not an option. It is a must. The things I learned in my first year as a Christian are still vital today. I still need to pray, but longer and with greater intensity and understanding. I still need to obey God's direction. Quickly and completely. These are the factors for growth. The basics are basic, and we never graduate from them. Morning prayer and Bible reading are not electives. They are required. Scripture memory and meditation on the Word are still vital to Christian development. And when the people of God see their leader slacking off in these matters, their confidence wanes. Their loyalty lags. Confusion replaces motivation. Lethargy replaces morale, and the enterprise begins to die.

Some years ago I was walking with a leader of a Christian mission. He was complaining to me that the men he had on his team were not following him. Some were not showing up for meetings. They weren't listening to him. Even in their spiritual discussions, the men seemed indifferent to his comments. They had tried to have a Bible study together, but the men began to show up late with their study half done or not show up at all. I zeroed in on this last point—Bible study—because the basics are still basic. I asked him how much time he had suggested as a minimum for study preparation.

"Two hours," he said.

"How much time are you putting in on yours?" I asked.

"Two hours," was his reply.

"You are not growing," I told him. "You were doing that ten years ago!"

I then challenged him to double the amount of time that he had set as a basic minimum in Bible study preparation. He took the challenge and began to double and at times triple his hours of investment in the Word. The men saw the difference, and their respect and commitment to his leadership took a dramatic turn. When I visited him a year later, I found a band of men committed to the task; their morale was high. The leader's personal spiritual growth was the key to the turnaround.

Enemies of Growth

1. *Pride.* Solomon wrote, "Pride goes before destruction, a haughty spirit before a fall" (Prov. 16:18). The proud person will be brought down. It is not a matter of *if* but *when.* It will happen either by his or her own repentance or the judgment of God on a bloated and haughty spirit. Nebuchadnezzar learned the hard way about pride going before destruction. We are told,

> Immediately what had been said about Nebuchadnezzar was fulfilled. He was driven away from people and ate grass like cattle. His body was drenched with the dew of heaven until his hair grew like the feathers of an eagle and his nails like the claws of a bird (Dan. 4:33).

He was a mighty leader of vast armies and hosts of people. Yet pride was his downfall. God will deal with leaders who refuse to give the glory to the One to whom it is due. He well knows how to remind us that "We have this treasure in jars of clay to show that this all-surpassing power is from God and not from us" (2 Cor. 4:7).

One of the greatest dangers of pride is that it implies overconfidence and in turn breeds a careless attitude toward spiritual realities. When leaders begin to place their confidence in themselves, they are on the brink of disaster. Their confidence must not rest in the gifts and abilities that God has given them. Yes, they may have a winsome personality, an ability to communicate, and the ability to win the loyalty and affection of others. But where did they get these? The Bible is clear. "For who makes you different from anyone else? What do you have that you did not receive? And if you did receive it, why do you boast as though you did not?" (1 Cor. 4:7).

I was once asked to conduct a weekend conference on discipleship at a lively and flourishing church. I was surprised to learn that just a few years ago the church was practically dead. Scores of the members of the congregation had walked off and joined other evangelical churches in the area. The problem was the pastor. Because he was not a man of prayer, he could not communicate to the congregation the principles that would help them become men and women of prayer. His shallowness in the Word showed up in shallow sermons and an inability to instruct the congregation in personal Bible study.

Finally, in desperation, the congregation fired the man and began to look for another. Soon they found a man who seemed to have the qualities they were looking for. No, he was not an eloquent preacher or even a very good teacher. He wasn't even a very good counselor. But one thing he had was a deep, sincere, intense love for Jesus Christ, which stemmed from his personal devotional life with the Lord. He was a man who prayed many hours and who feasted upon the Word for nourishment for his own soul. Soon after his arrival, a dramatic change began to occur. The congregation began to grow both in personal depth and in numbers. Some who had quit coming to church returned. People were won to Christ by members of the congregation and brought into the life of the church. Prayer meetings were well attended and real work for God was done as people made prayer a priority.

A dead, demoralized church was brought to life by a humble pastor. The secret? A man of God at the helm, whose total dependence was on God and who led the people into a dynamic fellowship with the Lord Himself. The former pastor relied on himself rather than rooting his ministry in prayer and dependence on God. But a man characterized by humble dependence on God was the catalyst the Holy Spirit used to lead the people to joy, devotion to God, and a desire to win others to Christ.

In your mind, picture a haughty spirit as an army general leading a great army toward the brink of ruin. Who do you see following along after him? Destruction. Bankruptcy. Defeat.Devastation. Annihilation. Catastrophe. Wreckage and the like. Now these are not just words out of *Roget's Thesaurus*. The parade that is led by pride and a haughty spirit is comprised of these things. Everytime. Everywhere. Pride and shame are shackled together with a fetter that cannot be broken by anyone but God. And He breaks it when repentance is evident.

Another prominent problem with pride is that it is in direct conflict with the first principle of wisdom, which is to fear the Lord.

Also, pride defies the great commandment of God to love Him and our neighbor. This puts proud people in an untenable position. They are in conflict with themselves, at odds with their neighbors, and in defiance of God. "The LORD detests all the proud of heart. Be sure of this: They will not go unpunished" (Prov. 16:5).

If leaders begin to think highly of themselves, they and the people with them will soon find themselves in trouble. If they come to the point where they begin to neglect the Lord and place their confidence in themselves, their growth will be stunted and they will begin to shrivel spiritually. And when people see this happening to their leaders, they will lose heart for the work of God.

Remember the words of Christ:

> Remain in me, and I will remain in you. No branch can bear fruit by itself; it must remain in the vine. Neither can you bear fruit unless you remain in me. I am the vine; you are the branches. If a man remains in me and I in him, he will bear much fruit; apart from me you can do nothing (John 15:4-5).

Effective outreach and service are not the result of overwork, but of overflow—the overflow of the life of intimate fellowship with Christ.

Sure, I'll be the first to admit that leaders can be effective if they apply the principles they learn from Dale Carnegie and Madison Avenue sales techniques. But this kind of effectiveness won't last in God's work. The songwriter was accurate when he wrote, "The arm of flesh will fail you." The Prophet Jeremiah wrote,

> This is what the LORD says: "Cursed is the one who trusts in man, who depends on flesh for his strength and whose heart turns away from the LORD. He will be like a bush in the wastelands; he will not see prosperity when it comes. He will dwell in the parched places of the desert, in a salt land where no one lives. But blessed is the man who trusts in the LORD, whose confidence is in Him. He will be like a tree planted by the water that sends out its roots by the stream. It does not fear when heat comes, its leaves are always green. It has no worries in a year of drought and never fails to bear fruit" (Jer. 17:5-8).

When the life of the leader begins to shrivel like a desert bush, the people who follow will begin to do likewise. We reproduce after our kind.

2. *Laziness.* If leaders are too lazy to pray, to study, to seek the Lord, they are once again on the brink of doom. Solomon spoke a clear word on this. "One who is slack in his work is brother to one who destroys" (Prov. 18:9). Lazy people destroy what they have. They let what they have sift through their fingers. They cast their God-given gifts and abilities to the wind.

I watched laziness take over in the life of a young man who had great potential for God. I met him when he was a seminary student, showing unusual promise. Most of his professors had high hopes for him. His keen mind, happy spirit, and communicative skills made him the talk of the seminary. Everyone was expecting him to go far. But I wasn't sure. I was working with him from another angle. I was trying to help him get established in the practice of morning prayer, Bible reading, and devotional meditation on the Word—the basics. However, he never quite conquered these areas. He was always too tired to leave his bed and go to his knees. His laziness was his downfall.

Twenty five years later, he was still in the same condition. A man who had potential for mighty things in the kingdom of God had sputtered along at a haphazard pace. He continued to pastor a flock of people who were sterile and powerless. They had not won a soul to Christ in years. The dynamics of discipleship remained foreign to their daily lives. They were not motivated to action, and their morale rested on the bottom rung of the ladder. The problem? A lazy leader. Solomon's words are to the point. The man who is too lazy to build is equally as destructive as the man who tears down what he has. He is brother to the one who is a great waster. If the leader neglects his responsibilities, he causes as much damage as the man who busies himself in wickedness. Both are destroyers.

In another proverb, Solomon spoke of the danger of sloth and the reward of diligence. "Do not love sleep or you will grow poor; stay awake and you will have food to spare" (Prov. 20:13). To love sleep is to abuse what God has ordained. Sleep must be used merely to prepare us for further service. Sleep should be the servant, not the master. The lover of sleep will turn into a listless, indolent, halfhearted individual who in no way resembles our Lord Jesus Christ, who did all things well and was consumed with zeal for God. The one who opens his or her eyes, and overcomes the lazy streak that plagues us all, is promised the satisfaction of the full life that comes from Christ, the Bread of God. Sleep can be a blessing or a curse.

One summer I visited a Navigator Training Program, arriving in time for breakfast. The trainees had been up for about two hours of calisthenics, morning devotions of Bible reading and prayer, and a few early chores. I looked around for the director and was told laughingly, yet somewhat cynically, that he was probably still asleep. I located his cabin and knocked on the door. Sure enough, when he opened the door, he was still in his robe. His eyes were half open, his voice was husky, and he was shocked and bewildered to see me standing there. I spent the day with the program and discovered that morale was plunging, and that motivation was weak. Before the day was out, I had the opportunity to share Proverbs 20:13 with the director. During the rest of the program, he worked to overcome his lazy streak, and because of his diligence won back the respect he had lost.

Allies of Growth

1. *Humility.* "The fear of the LORD teaches a man wisdom, and humility comes before honor" (Prov. 15:33). "Humility and the fear of the LORD bring wealth and honor and life" (Prov. 22:4)

It is clear from these verses that to walk humbly before God is absolutely necessary to spiritual growth. Such humility reveres the Lord and obeys His Word.

Many years ago, David Limebear, a close friend of mine from London, England, was touring America on holiday. My wife and I had him as a guest in our home in Colorado Springs. In a conversation one evening, David told of two groups of Christian leaders who had influenced his life. He spent three years around the first group. One person had a serious moral problem. One man was on the verge of deserting his wife and family. One was angry all the time. Another was fed up with life and was contemplating suicide. After David left this group, he joined the fellowship of some people who were quite the opposite. Their lives were a reflection of the character of God, and their homes were characterized by love and joy, patience and kindness.

As David reflected on these two groups, he was able to discern why they were different. The first group sat in judgment on the Bible. They approached its pages to pick it apart. The second group, however, had placed themselves under the authority of Scripture. They obeyed its teachings and claimed its promises.

The contrast was stunning. In pride, the first group set themselves up to judge the Bible. In humility the second group loved God's Word, and lived under its authority. They were experiencing the riches of the grace of God, and the Lord was honoring them. They had discovered life.

While David had been around the first group, his morale was zero and his motivation nil. However, David responded enthusiastically to the leadership of the second group, as they set him on the path of productive service for Christ.

Like David, most people respond to a humble leader. They are eager to follow such a leader, for they know the hand of God is on this person. They know that his walk with God will strengthen his convictions, strengthen his faith, and deepen his devotion to Christ, and that he will continue to grow.

2. *Godliness.* A person living in sin is obviously not growing in grace and in the knowledge of Christ. Growth comes as we learn the commands of God and by the power of the Holy Spirit apply them to our life. A psalmist said, "I will praise you with an upright heart as I learn your righteous laws. I will obey your decrees; do not utterly forsake me" (Ps. 119:7-8).

Godliness and growth are so interdependent that one promotes the other. They are virtues that walk hand in hand. Jesus commanded His followers to both learn and follow. To learn of Christ is to grow in His likeness. To follow Him is to live a godly life, to walk as He walked.

"The highway of the upright avoids evil; he who guards his way guards his life" (Prov. 16:17). All who walk the highway of God know that it leads closer and closer to His heart, His will, and His love. That's growth. That's the way to gain strength and stature in the work of God. The Prophet Isaiah had an incisive and interesting comment on this point: "And a highway will be there; it will be called the Way of Holiness. The unclean will not journey on it; it will be for those who walk in that Way; wicked fools will not go about on it" (Isa. 35:8).

What a promise! It doesn't matter where we start. We may have little education and few abilities. But if we are diligent in our pursuit of holiness on the highway of God, we will grow in both the wisdom and knowledge of the Lord.

Gifted leaders may start out with many advantages over their less endowed brothers and sisters. But if someplace along the road they become slack in their practice of godliness, their growth will soon be slowed and eventually brought to a halt. Leaders must therefore "keep their way" and look diligently to their inner desires and motivations. Growth is unmistakably connected to godliness. By guarding their moral behavior and shunning evil, leaders are also providing for the blessing of growth in grace and the knowledge of Christ.

If we want to keep growing, godliness must be our lifetime commitment. Note a further comment by Solomon: "Gray hair is a crown of splendor; it is attained by a righteous life" (Prov. 16:31). There is no glory in an evil old person. But the person who has walked the pathway of God for many years is encompassed by the glory of God. His or her wisdom is the result of a combination of study, application, and experience.

When you come right down to it, all the Lord requires of old men and women is that they be disciples. Young or old, the requirements are the same: faithfulness in the basics—in service and stewardship, and in devotion to Him.

Years ago, I had the privilege of chatting with Dr. Herbert Lockyer. He was anticipating his ninety-third birthday. My wife, Virginia, had baked him an apple pie and we were sitting in his living room enjoying the pie and discussing the things of the Lord. As I looked about the room of this aged saint, the evidences of a life of growth were everywhere. He pointed to the chair where he had his morning prayers. He noted his recent Bible study. His years were a crown of glory, for they had been lived in righteousness.

As I listened to him, I was reminded again that the only way to be found on the way of righteousness is to keep growing. If I don't do that, I will slide into the path of sin and be mired immobile in frustration and guilt.

3. *Prudence.* "The simple inherit folly, but the prudent are crowned with knowledge" (Prov. 14:18). Here growth and prudence are linked. Prudence is the ability to govern and discipline oneself by the use of reason. Although I must salt my life with periods of recreation and relaxation, the mainstream of my life must be lived among things that make for growth. And doing this is simply the exercise of prudent decisions and judgment. "The heart of the discerning acquires knowledge; the ears of the wise seek it out" (Prov. 18:15). Note that Solomon added the ear and the heart. What we hear can go in one ear and out the other. But when it lodges in the heart, it affects the life.

Prudence involves our attitude toward knowledge. Solomon had much to say about this attitude. "The discerning heart seeks knowledge, but the mouth of a fool feeds on folly" (Prov. 15:14). "He who listens to a life-giving rebuke will be at home among the wise. He who ignores discipline despises himself, but whoever heeds correction gains understanding" (Prov. 15:31-32).

Apollos was an interesting example of this attitude. We are told he had "thorough knowledge of the Scriptures." But we are also told that when Priscilla and Aquila heard him, "They invited him to their home and explained to him the way of God more adequately" (Acts 18:26). Imagine that! A preacher being taught by laypeople! It is amazing that they felt the freedom to *do* that. It is also amazing that Apollos had the humility and prudence to listen to them.

Prudent leaders will listen to the voice of their followers. In fact, they will create such a permissive atmosphere that the people feel free to talk to them, and are at ease in their presence. If they do this, they open the door to a wealth of information. This stimulates growth on their part and greater effectiveness in the task, which in turn helps maintain a high degree of morale and motivation.

In the spring of 1980, 162 leaders of The Navigators ministry gathered from around the world, to pray, plan, and ponder the direction of the ministry in the 1980s. Lorne Sanny, the president of The Navigators, led us in our morning sessions. He spoke to the group and then we broke up into discussion groups to talk about what he had said. The leaders of the groups noted the agreements and disagreements and brought them to the attention of Lorne and his leadership team. After a careful analysis of the feedback, Lorne incorporated the comments and suggestions of the discussion groups into his next morning's session. People were delighted to see their suggestions actually being meshed into the framework of the plans for the 1980s. Excitement ran high, and when the conference ended, it was evident that God was sending these leaders back to the four corners of the globe, motivated and committed to the task of helping fulfill Christ's Great Commission.

CHAPTER THREE

Be an Exemplary Leader

Some years ago I bought a chain saw. I had hopes of using it to cut limbs and logs for the fireplace. When I got it home, I took it to the garage, got it out of the box, and tried to assemble the thing. I read the operating manual carefully. The saw should have been relatively simple to put together; but the more I read, the more apprehensive and confused I became. The assembling guide referred to such things as housing, the guide ban, the lock-off button, the nose, and so on. For the life of me I couldn't figure out how to put it together.

Today my chain saw remains in the box, disassembled and useless. When the temperature is down in the 30s, and we've had our first snow, I'd really like to use the fireplace. But because I can't figure out the assembly instructions for my chain saw, everything is at a standstill.

The Marine Corps has a better system than written instructions only. In 1943, I enlisted in the Marine Corps and went to boot camp in San Diego. After the haircut, clothing issue, and a few days of running and calisthenics, I was issued a rifle. I knew nothing about firearms but knew that the Marine Corps would soon teach me to shoot it with some degree of accuracy. I was 18 years old, and thought the whole thing very exciting.

But the morning our drill instructor announced that we were going to learn to fieldstrip the rifle, I was terrified. The thought of taking that rifle apart, and trying to get it back together seemed too much for my nonmechanical mind. Along with everybody else, I began to undo the screws, and slide this and that in various directions, until I had in front of me a collection of bolts, screws, springs and odd-shaped pieces of metal. The drill instructor was very patient and very clear. Painstakingly, slowly, carefully, he led us through the exercise. He told us the name of each piece showing us where it fit. He left nothing to the imagination or chance. He led us through the project over and over again. Although most of the guys got the hang of it rather quickly, I didn't. I grew a bit discouraged and began to brood about the possibility that I would never make it as a marine. But the instructor kept at it, and so did I. After a number of methodical, step-by-step demonstrations and explanations, I began to catch on. Soon I could fieldstrip the M1 about as quickly as the rest. We had time competitions, and I began to finish near the top. I was elated.

Then came the shocker. Because there might come a time when we needed to take the rifle apart at night with no light, we were going to do it in time competition, *blindfolded!* Blindfolded? Yep, that was right. However, by this time I was up for it. I even had visions of winning. I was excited and eager. My turn came and I went at it with confidence and enthusiasm. Although I didn't win, I turned in a pretty good performance.

What made the difference between defeat with the chain saw and victory with the M1 rifle? Certainly not the complexity of the problem. The difference was the personal touch. With the one I merely had a set of instructions. With the other I had a concerned leader who was committed to teaching me something that one day might save my life in combat. I had a person there to help me—to explain and demonstrate the procedure in such a way that even I could grasp it. That's exactly what the people of God need in learning the life of discipleship—someone alongside to demonstrate and to help.

Need for Disciplers

Once when I was speaking at a weekend Navigator conference, I had lunch with one of our new staff members. He had recently graduated from seminary and was looking forward to a life of fruitful service for the Lord. We were having a discussion about the needs of new Christians. As we talked, he drew a simple diagram on a three-by-five-inch card he had in his shirt pocket. The diagram illustrated that there are different stages of Christian growth. It looked like this:

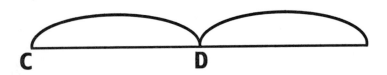

C   **D**

The C represented the point of conversion to Christ. The D represented the point in the Christian's life when he became a mature, committed, fruitful disciple. He explained to me that one of the problems he had encountered in seminary was that most of the students were taught to direct the content of their messages to people who were mature disciples. They were taught to present the fine points of Bible doctrine and the intricacies of the faith. But this type of preaching doesn't meet the needs of new Christians. They need to be shown how to master the basics that help them become the full-fledged New Testament disciples that Jesus talked about—people who are committed, who love each other, who are continuing in the Word and living fruitful lives. (See Luke 9:23; John 8:31; 13:34-35; 15:8.) Our staff member said he felt that these young men who were going out to pastor the flock assumed too much. They assumed that if people were simply *told* to pray, they would know how to pray; if they were told to study their Bible they would know how to do it; if they were told to witness they would begin to witness. He felt that people should be *shown* how to do these things. I agreed.

To hand people a Book with over 1,600 pages of fine print and no pictures, and assume they can master it and apply its teachings to their lives, is to assume too much. People need to be shown how. Jesus had to teach His own disciples how to pray. In fact, He gave them a pattern (Luke 11:1-4).

Dawson Trotman realized the importance of this. He would often remind us that telling is not teaching and listening is not learning. He gave us a five-step program to help a new Christian:
- Tell him what.
- Tell him why.
- Show him how.
- Help him get started.
- Help him keep going

And Daws would emphasize *show*. "Take him by the hand and lead him through it," he would say.

Need for Patterns

Shortly after I was discharged from the Marine Corps, I was converted to Christ. A few months later, I met Daws. You can imagine how his kind of teaching made so much sense to me. I recalled my drill instructor with his clear instruction and infinite patience and was able to see how that same pattern fit so well into the context of spiritual training.

One of the great needs in the church today is for patterns. All too often the pastor's sermons are directed to people who are disciples of Christ. But what about people who have not come to that point in their Christian growth? What steps can be taken to help them come to the assurance of their salvation? To help them establish the practice of prayer and Bible study? To help them learn how to bear witness for Christ—and eventually train others in these vital matters? Somehow these younger Christians must have their needs met. It seems obvious that what they need is a person who walks through the whole business with them.

If a lady is going to make a dress, what is the first thing she does? She goes down to the store and buys a pattern. Isn't that also the first need of a growing Christian? A pattern? The person has just emerged from darkness to light, from the power of Satan unto God. He has repented from sin and turned by faith to Jesus Christ. The Spirit of God has worked a miracle of grace in his life, and he is in a whole new world. "Therefore, if anyone is in Christ, he is a new creation; the old has gone, the new has come!" (2 Cor. 5:17). Now what? What's the first step? Where does he go from here? What does he need?

His need, of course, is for someone to teach him how to walk. "Whoever claims to live in him, must walk as Jesus did" (1 John 2:6) However, that does not come automatically. A person must learn to walk with God. But he cannot learn from some *thing,* He must learn from some *one.* When I sat down with my chain saw, I had some *thing*—I had a set of instructions. But when I sat down with my M1 rifle, I had some *one,* a patient, dedicated, concerned leader who was interested in me. Oh sure, all of those things you've heard about a marine drill instructor are true. He was tough. He was demanding. But he was also committed to taking a bunch of undisciplined, lazy, halfhearted civilians and making marines out of them. And he did. He was our pattern of a marine

Why do you think the Apostle Paul told Titus to show himself a pattern of good works? Why did he tell Timothy to be an example of good works? Why was he himself so diligent to set the example and show the way to others? Because that is the first need of people.

Need for Continuing Examples

It is not only the new Christian who needs an example to follow. All Christians need the *continuing* example of a godly life lived to the glory of God.

That is exactly what Jesus did for us. "To this you were called, because Christ suffered for you, leaving you an example, that you should follow in his steps" (1 Peter 2:21). When leaders set the kind of example that Christ set, they gain love and respect. Once at an evening service at our church, I talked with one of our ministers, the Rev. Bill Flanagan. He had just come back from El Paso, Texas, where he and a group of young men and women had spent three weeks helping out in a mission church. They had led the Vacation Bible School, taught Sunday School, and spent many long hours fixing up and painting the church. Bill looked a bit haggard, and I asked him if he were feeling okay. He said he had slept on the floor of the church with the rest of the gang for those three weeks, and on the trip back had gone without sleep for twenty-four hours. He had entered into the hardships with the group and they loved him for it. In spite of all the long hours and relative hardships, they returned to our church enthusiastic, and keenly motivated in the work of God. I'm sure that Bill Flanagan was one of the keys to this.

Bill, who heads up the singles' ministry of our church, asked me some years ago to lead the group in a "Day of Discipleship." We met early Saturday morning and went until late afternoon discussing the life of discipleship. During the lunch break, a few of the men and women gathered around and we talked about the dynamic of their group, which is one of the fastest-growing and most enthusiastic segments of our church. During the discussion I asked them why this was so. The answer was on the tips of their tongues—the life and example of Bill Flanagan.

"Oh sure, he is a good teacher," they assured me. "But the real secret is what he *is*, not what he says." Their eyes danced as they related to me various examples of his devotion to Christ and commitment to them as individuals—how he was available to them day or night, how he prayed for them, was patient with them, and accepted them into his life. At one time Bill was the Christian Education director for our whole church, but he resigned this position to direct the singles' ministry and give himself body and soul to them. They know this and love him for it. For Bill, this is a demanding job—long hours and many counseling sessions each week. Bill's cheerful spirit reflects the joy of the Holy Spirit in his life.

Bill's example to the singles of our church demonstrates the truth found in "A cheerful heart is good medicine, but a crushed spirit dries up the bones" (Prov. 17:22). Think about it. If on the trip to El Paso, Bill had slept on the floor, gone without sleep, and com- plained about it day and night, what would that have done to the people who were with him? Obviously, their motivation and morale would have plunged. Griping and complaining breeds more of the same, just as a cheerful spirit produces a cheerful spirit and a thankful heart.

Early one cold, wintry morning, I left the house with a bad attitude. The neighbor's dog had kept me awake most of the night. I was hungry and cold. I really didn't want to go the 6:30 A.M. prayer meet- ing that was scheduled for Lorne Sanny's team. When I arrived I was grouchy and sullen. In a few moments Lorne walked in. He told us of how the Lord had spoken to him recently from the Word about the importance of a joyful spirit and a thankful heart. He suggested we quote some verses on these topics. He started us off by quoting three or four that had had a profound effect on his life. He not only quoted verses about joy and thanksgiving—he communicated these qualities by the look in his eyes, the smile on his face, and the peace that radiated from his countenance. I was challenged, but remained silent. George Sanchez, Jack Mayhall, and Donald McGilchrist shared a few verses and discussed the implications of the passages.

Soon my heart began to thaw. I was convicted by it all, but mostly the things that Lorne was communicating by his attitude and demeanor. Solomon wrote, "As iron sharpens iron, so one man sharpens another" (Prov. 27:17). I experienced the sharpening influence of Lorne's example that morning, and God used it to help me in one of the major needs of my life.

If a leader remembers this truth, those who work with him or her will be affected and their own productivity for the Lord will be enhanced. I have noticed a definite change in my own life as the result of Lorne's example at that early morning prayer meeting—I find that I am more prone to look on the bright side than I was before. This, of course, has helped me in my witness for Christ. It is difficult to speak to another about a life of joy and victory in Christ when you are living in defeat in a crucial area of your own life. All of us need the continued example of a godly life.

Challenge Plus Know-How

There is power in a good example. We can learn things we never dreamed possible when *someone shows us how*. Professor Sid Buzzell, of the Christian Education department of the Dallas Theological Seminary, once asked me to teach a short course on leadership. During one of the lessons, I asked if there were a girl in the group who had never tied a man's necktie. One young lady raised her hand. I left the podium and walked over to her. I asked her to listen carefully as I explained this very simple process.

"First you hang the tie over your neck with the wide end on the right. Next you pull the wide end down until it is much lower than the narrow end. Then you swing the long wide part up through the gap left between your left wrist and the narrow end and throw it over the top, making sure that you keep a firm grip at the point where the narrow end and the top of the wide end meet. Then put the long wide end down through the V that is formed by the two ends. Then you again throw the long wide end over the top of the point where your thumb and index finger are grasping the top of the two ends, shove it up through the V, then down through the knot, then pull it to its full length, and straighten the knot."

After this clear, step-by-step explanation of a simple act, I asked her if she could tie a tie. She just looked confused.

Now let me ask you a question. Which is easier to learn: how to live as Christ's disciple and teach others to do the same or how to tie a man's necktie? Obviously, it is much simpler to learn to tie a necktie. But even that requires a simple demonstration in addition to an explanation. Within ten minutes I could have *shown* the young lady how to tie a tie. I would have given her one and I would have taken one. We would have stood before a mirror and I would have led her through the process a half dozen times. In fact, that's the way I taught my son, Randy, to tie his tie. But it took more than just telling him how. I went through it with him, step by step.

Challenge without know-how often leads to defeat, and defeat demoralizes. Time and again, new Christians are challenged to witness, pray, study the Bible, and so on. And time and time again, they try and then fail. Why? Because there is no one to show them how. But I have seen thousands of people won to Christ by colleagues of mine who then began to walk them through the life of discipleship *step by step*. And the new Christians quickly caught on. They watched, listened, tried it for themselves, and learned.

Just as defeat demoralizes, victory motivates. If leaders will take the time to lead their people through the steps of discipleship, they will have a victorious band of joyful, productive, motivated people whose lives bring glory to God and blessing to those around them.

CHAPTER FOUR

Be an Inspiring Leader

I knew something was different before I even got near the door of the barbershop. As usual the radio was on, but the mellow country-and-western tunes from our local station were gone. In their place was a brand of music that sounds something like a collision of 1,000 squawking ducks and 100 empty milk cans. When I walked through the door, the noise almost knocked me down. I sat in one of the empty chairs to wait my turn.

The two people who were cutting hair were strangers. Eldon, my barber of ten years, was nowhere in sight. Instead, there was a young man dressed in jeans and T-shirt, and a young lady in a long, baggy skirt, an embroidered blouse, and sandals. After a while, she called in my direction, "You're next."

When I sat down in the chair, she asked how I wanted my hair cut. I shouted over the noise that I just wanted it shortened up, with very little left on the sides. No sideburns. "Just a good, old-fashioned haircut." She seemed a bit puzzled, but she began. I could tell she had never done anything like that before. She proceeded to give me the sort of stylized haircut that she was used to, only modified a bit. I thought possibly she hadn't heard me over the blare of the radio, but I didn't say anything.

After she had been snipping away for several minutes, Eldon walked in and came to where I was sitting. It was obvious to him that I wasn't getting my standard haircut. He shouted to the girl that he would show her what I wanted. He raised the chair up to where he could reach my head, turned on the electric clipper and began to cut hair. The girl's eyes grew wider and wider. He took the hair around my ears right down to the skin. Then he chopped a batch off the top, explaining each move to her as he went along. Finally he stopped, turned to the girl, and suggested she finish it up. She smiled and said, "OK." She asked him how to get the chair back to her level, and once I was down where she could reach me, she did the final trimming. With some help from Eldon, she did a pretty good job.

This episode taught me a lesson. No number of years in beauty school can prepare a person for every customer. Sometimes a barber or beautician will run into a situation where he or she needs specific help.

This is true in the Christian life and ministry as well. Leaders need to make sure the people under them are continually growing. The *new Christian* needs the pure milk of the Word, lots of love, protection, the sense of belonging to the family of Christ, training in how to walk and talk, and so on. The *growing disciple* needs the discipline of the daily quiet time, consistent Bible study and Scripture memory, and help in learning how to witness and give his testimony. Also this person needs to be introduced to a lifestyle of serving others.

The *budding laborer* needs to be grounded in the great doctrines of the faith, deepened in his or her life of consecration and holiness, and sharpened in ministry skills. He or she also needs a bedrock commitment to the lordship of Christ and clear vision of the worth and potential of each individual. Finally, the *prospective leader* needs special training to prepare for the rigors of independent leadership. If these groups of people—the new Christians, the growing disciples, the budding laborers, and the prospective leaders—sense that they are under the care of people committed to help them grow and develop, their morale and motivation will be high.

At a gathering of 200 young leaders, I interviewed about half of them. One of the questions I asked was, "Why do you follow the man who heads up the mission in your area?" Three answers were given most often.

- The **vision** that the man was able to impart to them. He had communicated an exciting plan whereby their lives could become significant.

- The **availability** of their leader. When the young people needed counsel or help, the leader was there.

- The **commitment** of the leader. An overwhelming number of these young people said that the reason they followed the leader in their area was because they knew he was committed to help them grow and develop as people—in their spiritual lives. And that was the thing that kept them joyfully engaged in the task. Their motivation stemmed from the deep security that they were not being used, but rather were being helped and nourished, and were becoming better people. The leader was unreservedly committed to them.

He was committed to *their* welfare, not his; committed to *their* growth, not to his greed or self-glory; committed to *them*, not the task. And because they knew this, they joyfully marched together in the spiritual battle to help fulfill the Great Commission of Jesus Christ.

Qualities of a Leader

To maintain a high degree of motivation and morale, leaders must develop the people involved with them, helping their people to reach their fullest potential. And there are several practical things leaders can do to help their people grow. Solomon wrote of four qualities that are vital to a leader.

1. *Honesty.* Leaders must be absolutely honest with their people. "Better is open rebuke than hidden love. Wounds from a friend can be trusted, but an enemy multiplies kisses" (Prov. 27:5-6).

Like sheep without a shepherd, people are prone to wander. They need all the help they can get to stay on the right path. One of the marks of a good shepherd is that he watches over the sheep under his watchcare and does what he can to keep them from the poison weeds, the roaring lion, and the steep precipice.

Rebuke should begin in this same spirit of love and concern. *Open* rebuke means "speaking with free and unhindered honesty." Such honesty may sometimes hurt. However, I'm sure that any of us would rather have harsh treatment from a physician who could help us get well than gentle treatment from a doctor who could do us no good. A love that is too timid to help a person with his faults is not love at all. A love that wounds us is preferable to a love that neglects to draw us to the Lord. Love must not be silent when the life of a person is at stake. This, of course, is one of the burdens of leadership. But if people know the leader will shoot straight with them and help them when they need it, their morale and motivation will stay up, and their lives can be developed.

One summer I visited one of our summer training programs at the Maranatha Bible Camp near North Platte, Nebraska. As I looked over the program and got to know the teams, I wondered if our program director had made a mistake. One of the team leaders was a matter-of-fact, hard-nosed, plain-spoken individual. On his team were six men who were rather introverted. I was afraid this team leader would drive them further into themselves, and was planning to talk to the program director about it to suggest a switch. However, I just didn't have the freedom from the Lord to do so. I left the program a bit concerned and made this team a matter of definite prayer.

After a few weeks, I returned to the camp to see how things were going. To my happy surprise, I discovered that the team for which I had been concerned was the one the program director felt had the highest morale and esprit de corps. During my stay I talked with the six team members and asked how they liked the program, and how they were getting along with their team leader. They said they appreciated the program and really got along well with their leader. I asked them why they held him in such high esteem. What had he done to win their confidence and respect? The thing they appreciated was the fact that he did not pussyfoot around with them. He was always straightforward and fair. He commended them enthusiastically, but was not afraid to lay it on the line when they needed correction. To put it simply, he was honest with them. They were a cheerful, motivated team, and very thankful to the Lord for the privilege of being trained by an open, honest leader. "He who rebukes a man will in the end gain more favor than he who has a flattering tongue" (Prov. 28:23).

2. *Loyalty.* Leaders must stay with the person through thick and thin. They cannot walk off when the person fails in his or her responsibilities or suffers a spiritual setback. "A friend loves at all times, and a brother is born for adversity" (Prov. 17:17). Leaders care and stand by their people.

I spent the summer of 1976 in Washington, D.C. One of my
responsibilities was to conduct witnessing workshops in various
churches in the Washington/Baltimore area. One of these was the
Evergreen Baptist Church, a black congregation, located in the
heart of downtown D.C. When I arrived at the church on a
Monday night, I visited with a deacon who was standing outside
on the sidewalk. As we talked, a young lady walked by and the
deacon called to her. He reminded her that there was a service at
the church that night. She explained that her mother was sick, and
she had to care for her. After a rather lengthy conversation with the
girl, he seemed satisfied that she was in fact going to take care of
her mother and was not just putting up an excuse to miss church.
As the girl walked off, he turned to me and said, "They know that
if they don't come to church, I will come and get them."

Now that's concern. That's a caring heart of a leader fulfilling his
responsibilities. He showed concern for the people in his church
even when they weren't concerned about the church. He loved
them whether they were doing right or wrong, whether they were
living in victory or in sin. Adversity will cement a good leader's
love for people, rather than dislodge it. When the disciples for-
sook Jesus and fled, did He forsake them? Absolutely not. "Jesus
knew that the time had come for him to leave this world and go
to the Father. Having loved his own who were in the world, he
now showed them the full extent of his love" (John 13:1).

Jesus' love for us today is just as constant, for He is touched with
the feeling of our infirmities. Jesus stays with us in fair weather
and foul. When people see a leader manifesting this Christlike
trait, their loyalty is firm, their commitment remains solid, and
their morale stays high.

This does not mean that their commitment and involvement will
never lapse. Even the Apostle Peter failed at one point in his
commitment to follow Christ. But through the unswerving love of
Christ, Peter came to a place of loyalty and devotion that was so
unshakable God could use him to encourage others in their hour
of trial. To people who were being falsely accused of being
evildoers, he wrote, "Dear friends, do not be surprised at the
painful trial you are suffering, as though something strange were
happening to you" (1 Peter 4:12). Peter came to the place where

he could follow Christ through thick and thin, and maintain a cheerful spirit in it all. Even after merciless beatings, Peter and the other leaders left "the Sanhedrin, rejoicing because they had been counted worthy of suffering disgrace for the Name" (Acts 5:41). They were unswerving in their devotion to the One who loved them and gave Himself for them. Christ's example led the apostles to respond in kind. Their loyalty was firm, their commitment was solid, and their morale remained high.

3. *Generosity.* Leaders should commend work that is well done. We all need a pat on the back now and then, and a word of encouragement. But praise can have either a good or a bad effect. "The crucible for silver and the furnace for gold, but man is tested by the praise he receives" (Prov. 27:21).

Praise is a great tester of character. If people are filled with vanity, if they crave self-glory and hunger for recognition, praise will do nothing but fan the flame of their weaknesses. On the other hand, if they are humble and wise, a word of praise can be used by the Lord to stimulate them to even greater service for Christ. Therefore, leaders must know their people and treat each one according to his or her individual needs.

As people assume more leadership responsibility, the leader training these people must teach them to watch out for the dangers of praise and adulation. If young leaders are doing a good job, they can be bombarded mercilessly by the praise of people. Therefore, they must learn to walk a fine line at this point, and accept kind remarks in a spirit of humble grace. But in their souls they must beware of letting others place on them even for a moment the crown that only Christ is worthy to wear. Well-meant but overdone compliments need to be dealt with in the power of the Holy Spirit. No one can do it alone.

As leaders work to develop the lives of the Christians they are responsible for, they must be governed by basic principles.

- They should be careful in giving praise. Self-love dies hard and leaders can do their brothers and sisters great damage by heaping praise on those who can't handle it. It is no act of love to place weak brothers or sisters under the frown of God.

- They should teach others how to accept praise for what it is—
  an honest attempt to be encouraging. But they should also
  recognize the fact that the Devil can slip in a drop of poison
  and do leaders tremendous harm. Praise can be doubly hard
  to handle if leaders have worked hard and given their best.

- They must teach others they are only channels. It is Christ in
  them who gives strength and Christ though them who accomplishes the task.

Just as silver and gold are tested by the furnace, so a person is
tested by praise. Saul and David both went through the crucible of
praise. "As they danced, they sang: 'Saul has slain his thousands,
and David his tens of thousands'" (1 Sam. 18:7). One failed and
one weathered the test. Praise, therefore, is that which the vain
leader seeks and the weak leader is hurt by. The true character of
a leader is manifested by how he or she handles praise.

I was once talking with a junior executive in a large corporation.
He told me of an incident that took place in his company, and of
the effect it had on his motivation and morale. He had been at his
desk late one night and had come in early the next morning. His
workload was heavy and he was feeling a bit sorry for himself.
About midmorning, the phone rang. To his utter amazement, it
was the president of the corporation. He had just called to tell the
junior executive how much he appreciated all he was doing and
to commend him for the excellence of his work. The president's
voice was sincere and the man could tell that he really meant
what he was saying. The president inquired about my friend's
family, how things were going at home, the state of his health,
and so on. After a leisurely chat, the president hung up. When my
friend told me the story, he looked me in the eye and said, "You
know, I really love that man. It means a lot to get an honest pat
on the back once in a while."

4. *Humility.* In all of their efforts, leaders must remember that God is
doing the training in the lives of the people. "The crucible for silver
and the furnace for gold, but the LORD tests the heart" (Prov. 17:3).

For a number of years, I was directly involved in our Navigator
summer training programs. We would prayerfully plan the

programs, select the staff, and choose the trainees. For five to ten weeks we would be together, involved in work projects, Bible studies, preaching sessions, small group discussions, and one-on-one times with the trainees.

In each program we had clear objectives. One program would be geared to evangelism. Another would major on Bible study. Another would have missions as its main emphasis. And so on. Toward the end of the sessions, the leaders would gather the gang together for a time of reflection and testimony to find out what they had learned. It was amazing to see that in many cases, the main benefit they received from the programs was in no way related to the emphases. God had spoken to them in their quiet time or Bible study and had changed their lives. We learned something from this—we should do our best to develop the people, but always remember that God's training program is running simultaneously with ours.

In every aspect of life, God is the One who works in lives to train people, and leaders must let the Lord do His work. If a leader observes one of the flock going through some tough times, there's the tendency to step in and try to carry the person through—to play God for the person. This is a mistake. The picture in Proverbs 17:3 is of metal in the refiner's furnace. If it does not go in the furnace, the dross will remain ingrained in the metal forever. Outward polishing will not solve the problem. The need is for fire. No mild solution will suffice. The evil that lurks within the hearts of men must be brought to the surface and thrown away. Leaders should pray for their people, committing them to the tenderness, love, and wisdom of God. And then leaders should let God do His work.

Priorities for a Leader

There are two additional principles that are particularly helpful when developing prospective leaders.

1. *Choose wisely*. The initial key to developing prospective leaders is careful selection of the right persons.

It is a double tragedy to spend time preparing a person for a leadership responsibility only to discover that you have chosen the wrong person. You have only one life to invest, and to give it to the wrong people is a waste. Also, to have to go to a person and admit your mistake, and help redirect the course of his or her life can be devastating. Because this person's heart was set on a leadership position, he or she can easily be shaken in self-confidence, confidence in your leadership, and confidence in God. It might take months or years to heal the wounds that result from that kind of spiritual injury. So pick the person carefully and prayerfully. Remember, Jesus spent time in prayer before choosing the Twelve (Luke 6:12-13).

As you look for the trainee, keep in mind that some people respond to instruction, reproof, and correction, while others don't. "Do not rebuke a mocker or he will hate you; rebuke a wise man and he will love you. Instruct a wise man and he will be wiser still; teach a righteous man and he will add to his learning" (Prov. 9:8-9). Some people are ready for help and counsel, and others are not. But it goes deeper than that—some people have the capacity to be trained as leaders, and others don't.

2. *Invest time.* The second key, once you have carefully selected the man or woman whom you believe God wants to develop into a leader, is to spend individual time with that person. "Iron sharpens iron, so one man sharpens another" (Prov. 27:17). This is a vivid picture for anyone raised on a farm. I can still see my dad standing there with his strong-tempered steel file sharpening the hoe, the scythe, the corn knife, and the long-handled shovel. And in this I see an excellent picture of the intense personal contact that is needed to prepare prospective leaders for their job.

Some years ago I had the privilege of being under the tutelage of one of the most productive Christian leaders in the United States. One day we were riding in a car together. I began to criticize a group of Christians and a project in which they were engaged. I had heard someone else talk about their effort, and was parroting what I had heard. Dick sat quietly for awhile, and then turned to me and began to ask me some rather pointed questions. "How much do you actually know about it? Is your information first or second hand? Do you have all the facts? For instance, are you aware of this? And this?"

I began to squirm and I am sure my face turned red from embarrassment. When I tried to weasel out of the situation, he forced me to be honest. After I had made a complete fool of myself, he took a few minutes to tell me the truth of the matter. Then he opened the Scriptures and shared with me what the Bible had to say about my actions. I was chagrined—but wiser, and I learned a valuable lesson. God used that incident, along with a few others that summer, to file down some rough edges in my life.

Possibly you are saying, "But I'm not a sharp individual. Can God use me to sharpen others?" Of course! But first He must sharpen you. One way God sharpens is through other people. Make yourself a student of men and women who are being used by the Lord. You will learn more by studying people than by studying books. Learn to ask questions. Ask these people over to dinner, out to lunch, to play a game of golf or tennis. Spend time with people and study them. Learn by observation. The Spirit of God will use other people to temper and strengthen you and make you a great sharpening instrument in His hands.

God gives leaders the responsibility to develop the people committed to their charge. Without exception, every person under a leader's charge needs further development and training. Each one has been given a gift by God—a gift that the Spirit of God uses to enrich and deepen the lives of others, which serves to build up the body of Christ.

CHAPTER FIVE

Be an Efficient Leader

Last year after our first snowstorm, I decided I needed a new sweater. Since my blue one had holes in both elbows, and my brown one had shrunk, it was time to find a good warm sweater to see me through the winter.

When I arrived downtown, I saw that one of our oldest and best stores was having a giant sale. But more than that—the store was going out of business.

As I was looking through the sweaters, one of the salesmen came over and began to chat with me. I expressed my surprise that the store was closing and asked the reason. He looked at me with a sad smile, and said two words: "Poor management."

I have heard those words so many times. Poor management is one of those behind-the-scenes problems that generally surfaces after it is too late to do anything about it. However, leaders can avoid such problems by knowing and applying the key principles of good management.

Lorne Sanny is the one who first shared these keys with me. I know their value in the international ministry of The Navigators. Let's look at these principles from the context of Scripture.

Receive Direction

The leader's first step is to get a clear signal from God as to what he wants done. If the leader is doing the will of God, the way He wants it done, and where He wants it done, that leader will be motivated for the task. An awareness that he or she is involved in the will of God can have an electrifying effect on the leader's soul and spirit.

Years ago I was talking with a man who had been in Christian work for a number of years. His morale had hit bottom and his motivation was nil. He had been in the midst of a big program, working feverishly day and night. Slowly, it began to dawn on him that in spite of all the clanging and banging of the noisy church machinery that spun madly through the week, very little was actually being produced for the kingdom of God. For months he had been swept along at a frantic pace.

When we talked, he began to express his deepest inner feelings. He was filled with doubts and uncertainties. In the eyes of the rest of the Christian community, he was a glowing success, a man to be admired, even envied. But he himself was in a dark and lonely world of doubt. What was it really all about? Was this frantic activity the essence of the Christian ministry? If so, maybe he just didn't fit. He had thought of a number of options. Maybe he should leave the church and follow one of them. He was frustrated and depressed.

Finally, I was able to break into his flood of words. "How much time are you giving to prayer?"

"Not much," he said.

"How much?" I asked.

"Practically no time at all," was his admission.

So we talked about that for a while. By adjusting a few items on his schedule, we were able to find a day when he could drive out by the lake and spend a day alone with the Lord.

We then talked about his Bible study. He admitted it was usually a last-minute endeavor to put some sermons together. Again we raked through his schedule, to arrange some time for personal, devotional Bible study, oriented to application in his own life. He agreed that this was just what he needed, and vowed to make diligent effort to set aside regular time for prayer and the study of the Word—not primarily for the ministry to others, but to refresh his own soul and spirit.

As the months passed, he stuck with the changed schedule.

As a result of his renewed fellowship with God, his motivation and enthusiasm returned. Also, he had a new perspective on his ministry, and developed a deeply settled assurance that he was in the will of God. Naturally, the change affected the church, as its program became less frantic and more productive. Because this pastor was closer to God, he was able to help his people more effectively. His sermons and his public prayers were richer. He was a new man, and his people rose up and called him blessed.

A friend of mine told me about a missionary who was trying to decide whether to go back to the field. He had left the mission station in defeat. The work had been hard, and opposition had made life unbearable. There had been little fruit and much persecution. One of the Christians in his village had been tortured; and as a result of the beatings and inhumane torture, he had emerged from the jail blind and broken in body.

The missionary was in a quandary—should he return to the field or not? What did God want him to do? To test the leading of God, he wrote on his visa application that he was going to the country to preach the Gospel of Jesus Christ and to win souls for the Lord. He was sure that it would take a miracle for a visa containing that sort of information to be approved.

However, to his utter amazement, it came through. He believed this was of God, and as a result, he gained a new vision for the work, and new excitement about returning. Yes, the climate was still hot and muggy. The housing was still inadequate. Yes, the government was still on a rampage against Christians, and there were still reports of harassment. Trials and afflictions probably awaited him. Yes, he was aware that results might still be meager. But now there was another factor in the equation. He was *convinced* it was what God wanted him to do. And he was filled with keen expectation of what God was going to do.

On returning to the village, he found the people very responsive to the Gospel. While he was away, they had felt a profound sense of shame and disgrace for their part in the persecution. The Christian convert who had been blinded and broken in body had died, and God had used his death to stir within their hearts an unusual readiness to hear the Gospel. At last report, 500 former enemies of Christ were in Sunday School classes studying the Word of God. This missionary had received clear leading from God that he should return. The promise that God made through Solomon had proven trustworthy: "He will make your paths straight" (Prov. 3:6).

Communicate with Your People

Once leaders know what God wants them to do, they must clearly communicate God's direction to the people and help them see how they fit into the undertaking. This is the second key to effective management. All people involved in the enterprise must know what their jobs are—what the leader wants them to do.

Moses followed this principle when building the tabernacle. God revealed His will to Moses in clear and explicit terms: "Then have them make a sanctuary for me, and I will dwell among them" (Ex. 25:8). He went on to say, "Set up the tabernacle according to the plan shown you on the mountain" (Ex. 26:30). And it wasn't long before Moses gathered the people together and passed along the Word of God to them. "Moses assembled the whole Israelite community and said to them, 'These are the things the LORD has commanded you to do'" (Ex. 35:1).

Nehemiah is another example of this process. After God revealed His will to him, Nehemiah was soon in Jerusalem sharing it with the people:

> Then I said to them, "You see the trouble we are in: Jerusalem lies in ruins, and its gates have been burned with fire. Come, let us rebuild the wall of Jerusalem, and we will no longer be in disgrace." I also told them about the gracious hand of my God upon me and what the king had said to me (Neh. 2:17-18).

What happened here? These people had been sitting around looking at a broken-down wall for years. What got them excited about starting this great building project? They had a motivated leader, a man whom God had sent to get the job done. When Nehemiah told them what God had said, and that the king was behind the project, the people became excited.

If leaders want to maintain their own morale, and that of their people, let them first discern the will of God for themselves. Then they must make sure that everyone who works with them knows where they fit in the project, and exactly what is expected of them.

A man said to me, "My boss thinks I'm a mind reader. Recently, he handed me a project and said, 'Work on this.' I did my best and gave it back to him.

"'That's no good,' he said and gave it back to me to work on again. I tried it from a completely different angle and took it back to him. He was still dissatisfied. So I tried the third time but to no avail. He still didn't like it. The project is still unfinished and I still don't have a clue what it is he wants me to do with the thing."

As I listened to the man, I could tell his enthusiasm and motivation for the project were at rock bottom. I had known him for years and believed he was well able to complete the project if only the boss would tell him exactly what he wanted.

Solomon was a man who did just that. When he needed some timber for the temple project, he went to Hiram and explained what he needed and why. Hiram took the project and finished it in good order.

Later, when Solomon needed some metal work done, he spoke to Hiram about it. Again Hiram's response was positive and the project went off well. The key to it all was clear directions to a qualified man. (See 1 Kings 5 and 7.)

Delegate Responsibility

After Moses led Israel out of Egypt, he was working himself to a frazzle. Jethro, his father-in-law, gave him some sound advice.

> But select capable men from all the people—men who fear God, trustworthy men who hate dishonest gain—and appoint them as officials over thousands, hundreds, fifties and tens. Have them serve as judges for the people at all times, but have them bring every difficult case to you: the simple cases

they can decide themselves. That will make your load lighter, because they will share it with you (Ex. 18:21-22).

The key phrase here is, "And *let them* judge the people at all times." The leader must first give the followers a job, and then let them do it. All too often a leader will delegate a job, and then meddle and fuss to the point where he or she has actually taken the task away from the person. This is a classic mistake.

Some years ago, when I was in the middle of a rather large ministry assignment for The Navigators, I sat down with a competent and dedicated man who was working with me and began to share an idea that would involve him in the project.

After several minutes he stopped me and said, "There is no point in your telling me this."

I was quite taken back and asked why. Was it because he had no interest in it, or was he simply refusing to help?

"No," he said, "it's nothing like that. It is simply that I have watched you, LeRoy, and I know that if I took the project, you wouldn't let me do it. You would poke your nose in, fuss around, begin to change this and that, and pretty soon the rug would be out from under me and you would be doing it yourself."

I argued with him, trying to justify myself. But I came to the point where I had to admit that he was right.

"*Let them* do it." This is a key to motivation and morale. However, there is one qualification to the principle. If the leader wants to release his or her hands from the reins and let another person get on with the job, he or she must first select and train the right person for the job. Whether he or she is choosing people to provide leadership or to do manual work, a leader should make sure they are able people whom God has qualified for the task.

Solomon had a word of wisdom on this point: "A king delights in a wise servant, but a shameful servant incurs his wrath" (Prov. 14:35). The leader needs to choose a *wise* and *able* helper. "Like a bad tooth or a lame foot is reliance on the unfaithful in times of trouble" (Prov. 25:19). Unfaithful people are a source of pain and discomfort. They will collapse under pressure. So let the leader consider well the consequences of the question, "Will you let me do it?" lest he or she be forced to rely on people who are not able to perform.

Be available

The fourth key is contained in the question, "Will you help me when I need it?" To review, the leader must first get direction from God. Then the people must know what they are supposed to do. They need the confidence that once they take on a job, the leader will let them do it.

But they also need the quiet confidence that the leader will be available when they need help. This is true regardless of age, ministry, or position in the church of God.

A few years ago, I was at a conference on the West Coast. After I had finished speaking at the Saturday night meeting, a young man stopped me and asked if he could talk with me. I explained to him that I already had made an appointment with another man, but he persisted. "Don't you have just a little time?"

"Well," I said, "we could talk on the way over to the building where I am meeting him."

"Fair enough," he said. He then began to pour out a tale of woe to me that was heartrending. He was in a mess spiritually. He had been a Christian for three years and during those years had become very active in a Christian organization. He had really gotten involved and had experienced good success, and that's when his problems began. He began to give, give, and give. Give his time . . . spend long hours . . . pour out his life. But in doing so, his life became shallow and his endurance was stretched to the limit. Finally, he could go on no longer and just gave up. When he heard that I was going to be at the conference, he drove down in the hope that we could talk. He was absolutely burned out and there was no one to whom he could go for help.

In the few minutes we had, I talked with him about how to become rooted and built up in Christ and established in the faith.

As I reflected on the event afterward, I was pained in my spirit. Here was an eager young Christian with a real problem and no one to turn to. And when he heard that there was someone a few hundred miles away who might be able to help, he took the chance that I might have time available, and he made the trip. Solomon said, "A friend loves at all times, and a brother is born for adversity" (Prov. 17:17). A leader should be a friend who is there in time of need.

Yes, let the people do the work. Don't interfere and don't pester them. But always give them the assurance that you are available and eager to help when they need you.

Evaluate Regularly

The fifth key is embodied in the question, "Will you tell me how I'm doing?" It is demoralizing not to know what your leader thinks about your performance.
- "Is it okay?"
- "Is my boss satisfied?"
- "Does my boss like what I am doing?"

If these questions are not answered periodically, people's minds can become consumed with suspicion, imagination, and confusion. When that happens, work slows and possibly stops because people are demoralized.

I have seen this so many times in my visits to various areas of ministry, both in the U.S. and abroad. Once I was with a friend who reports to a man in another city. As we talked, he brought up this very subject. "I really don't have a clue if what I am doing is what the boss wants," he said. Then he looked at me and said in a rather plaintive way, "Perhaps you could talk with him, explain what I am doing, and see if he is satisfied."

I had before me a man whose morale was low and whose enthusiasm for the ministry was lower still. He seemed cut off and in the dark. His mind was in a turmoil. Was he going to be replaced? He told me about the mental arguments he had had with his boss, as he imagined all sorts of things. I did what I could to get the two men together, to ease my friend's mind, and to help the leader see his responsibilities to evaluate the man's work and honestly tell him how he was doing.

A contrast to this is the way Lorne Sanny handles those of us on the international headquarters team who report to him. We each update our job description and priority objectives every six months. Periodically, Lorne will call me into his office and discuss these with me point by point. "It looks like you're okay here, but these items probably need a little more work," he will say. Then we share something from the Word together, have a prayer, and I leave the office knowing exactly where I stand with him. It's a great feeling and it does much to keep me motivated.

When leaders evaluate the work of their people, they *must* have the facts, and know what they are talking about. Leaders can profit from the truth in Proverbs 10:31: "The mouth of the righteous brings forth wisdom." Nothing demoralizes the people more than to realize their leader really doesn't know what is going on.

Summary

Moses applied these principles of effective management. How did they affect the morale and motivation of the people? One of the best tests of morale among the people is the way they give their time and money to the work of the Lord. If they are disgruntled, disillusioned, and disenchanted, they give little. But if they are fired up about what God is doing in them, among them, and through them, they give in abundance. In light of that, note Exodus 36:4-7:

> The skilled craftsmen . . . left their work, and said to Moses, "The people are bringing more than enough for doing the work the LORD commanded to be done."
> Then Moses gave an order and they sent this word throughout the camp: "No man or woman is to make anything else as an offering for the sanctuary." And so the people were restrained from bringing more, because what they already had was more than enough to do all the work.

The work was hard. The hours were long. The living conditions were less than ideal. But the people were motivated and morale ran high.

Leaders should remember to ask:
- Do I have clear direction from God?
- Do I tell my people what they are supposed to do?
- Do I let them do it?
- Do I help them when they need it?
- Do I tell them how they are doing?

Management concerns itself primarily with people—not things. These five questions are vital. They must be answered. More than that, they must be lived out in everyday life. And when they are, the motivation and morale of the people will be secure.

CHAPTER SIX

Be a Caring Leader

There are various kinds of shepherds and their ideas on sheep tending are not the same. Let's look at two different types of shepherds.

The first type of shepherd is more a gatherer than a tender of sheep. These shepherds are forever out beating the bushes. They will find a few sheep and then run them into the sheepfold. But their personal *care* for the sheep is minimal. After they get them into the sheepfold, they lose interest in them. Sensing this, the sheep often wander out the back door and get lost. But this does not seem to bother these shepherds all that much. Daybreak finds them out in the bushes again whacking away; by nightfall they have a few more to add to the fold. However, after a while, some of these also wander off like others before them. As a result, there is very little numerical growth in the flock, and the sheep that *do* stick around are not well nourished. These flocks are sickly rather than strong and robust.

The second type of shepherd has a different idea as to how to go about it. Yes, these shepherds are as eager to add new ones to the flock, but they give a great deal of attention to the sheep after they are in the fold—diligent, personal attention.

All of us at one time met someone who searched us out and led us into the sheepfold. But our needs did not end there. We needed lots of tender care. We needed to be nourished in the words of faith. Because our problems were unique, we also required individual personal attention. The key to this was not the sheep but the shepherd.

What do shepherds need to keep the sheep healthy, producing, and reproducing? A number of things are profitable, but two are absolute necessities.

The first essential is a clear understanding of the basic needs of sheep. Shepherds must diligently study this, then look over the flock, and determine what their sheep need.

The second essential is their diligence and drive to do whatever is necessary to meet those needs. Solomon articulated it beautifully: 'Be sure you know the condition of your flocks, give careful attention to your herds" (Prov. 27:23). In other words, find out what needs to be done and *do it!*

Notice Solomon spoke directly to shepherds. It is their business to know how the sheep are doing. This is not something they can delegate. The Apostle Paul understood this clearly: "Paul said to Barnabas, 'Let us go back and visit the brothers in all the towns where we preached the word of the Lord and see how they are doing'" (Acts 15:36). He and Barnabas had completed their missionary journey. Many had come to Christ, as sheep brought into the fold. Now the great apostle proposed a visit to see how things were with them. Were they being fed and cared for? Were the shepherds doing their job? Was there any way he could help? His concern was intense. To the Thessalonians he said, "For now we really live, since you are standing firm in the Lord" (1 Thes. 3:8). If they were doing well, his spirit soared with life. But if they were in trouble—sick, hungry, mistreated, succumbing to their proneness to wander—something in him died. His very life was tied to their welfare.

Solomon called on shepherds to be diligent. Haphazard sloth is not acceptable. There is too much at stake. Think of the potential of a healthy flock growing and multiplying forever! Diligence is the order of the day.

Some years ago, Randy, Virginia, and I were flying from Belgrade, Yugoslavia, to Warsaw, Poland. We arrived at the airport only to discover that the flight was being delayed for about six hours. Randy went immediately to the office of the agent of Yugoslavian Air Lines to get the story and find out what we should do. The agent was full of apologies. It seems there was a group in a town a few hundred miles away who was also going to Warsaw. So the airlines simply sent our plane off to get them. So there we sat. The agent went into action. He arranged a nice meal for us at his expense. He gave us our boarding passes in advance to ensure us seats on an already overbooked flight and had our passports stamped ahead of time so we wouldn't have to stand in the long line at flight time. He also told us to remain in the waiting room until he came and escorted us onto the plane.

When departure time came, he was nowhere to be seen. But we waited. Mobs of people scrambled through the door and hurried to the plane. Finally, he came and walked to the plane with us. When I looked inside the plane, my heart fell. All the seats were taken. But at that moment he unlocked a door leading to the rear of the plane and there was a six-seat first-class section. He ushered us in and spoke to the stewardess, telling her to take good care of us. He was a good shepherd. We were his little flock and he took pains to see we were well cared for. We were on an old, Russian, four-engine propeller plane, filled with loud, happy, pushing, shoving travelers, but we had a quiet, peaceful ride. The agent was diligent to look out for our welfare.

After that trip, I took a domestic flight that was a sharp contrast. The steward came by and offered me coffee. I asked if I could have some hot tea.

"Of course," he said, "I'll be right back with some." Sometime later he came by to offer me some more coffee.

"No thanks," I said. "I was hoping to have a cup of tea."

"Oh, good grief," he exclaimed. "I completely forgot. I'll be right back." He never came back.

One shepherd was diligent, the other was not.

Enemies of Pastoral Care

What will keep a shepherd from exercising that diligence? It seems to me that four things are enemies of conscientious care from the shepherd.

1. Self-centeredness. Jesus spoke to this trait:

> The thief comes only to steal and kill and destroy; I have

come that they may have life, and have it to the full. I am the good shepherd. The good shepherd lays down his life for the sheep. The hired hand is not the shepherd who owns the sheep. So when he sees the wolf coming, he abandons the sheep and runs away. Then the wolf attacks the flock and scatters it. The man runs away because he is a hired hand and cares nothing for the sheep (John 10:10-13).

Note what the thief and the hireling have in common. They are self-centered, filled with greed and desire for personal gain. Their commitment is toward enhancing their own welfare at the expense of the sheep.

You may wonder why the hireling is involved with the sheep at all. He is there for the money. It's merely a job. When the going gets rough, he runs away.

Are there pastors, missionaries, and Christian workers today who look on the ministry as a means of personal glory or self-gain? Who regard the ministry as just another profession? Yes, there undoubtedly are. But thank God they are in the minority.

Unfortunately, the thief and hireling will always be with us. And may God help the poor flock that is plagued by such a person.

2. *Ignorance.* There is a devastating passage in the Old Testament that speaks to this: "The shepherds are senseless and do not inquire of the LORD; so they do not prosper and all their flock is scattered" (Jer. 10:21).

The prophet put his finger on the heart of the problem. If shepherds are out of fellowship with the Lord, their lives will not bless the sheep. There are many reasons for this.

- Shepherds are really only a channel through whom the Lord communicates His blessing to the sheep. Their need for God is greater than their need for the channel. If leaders are not walking with the Lord in the light of His Word, their ministry will be dead.

- If leaders are not studying the Word, they will never learn what the sheep need or how to truly minister to their lives.

The ignorance of leaders will be a curse to the flock. Wise leaders will not only know the general needs of their people, but will also be able to determine the current specific needs of their people.

I once talked with Lorne Sanny about one of his men. I told him I thought there was something that had happened in this man's department that he should be aware of. However, Lorne cautioned me against sharing it at this time. "Wait until his next meetings are over. He has quite a bit on his mind these days."

I was challenged. Lorne is a man with a global responsibility, but he has the time and inclination to keep up to date with the men who report to him—even though they are scattered to the four winds. This is exactly what Solomon was pleading for. He urged the shepherds to exercise diligence to know the state of their flocks. This is no easy task. There is much false and unbalanced religious teaching today through books, magazines, radio, and television. Pastors must keep abreast of what their flock is feeding on. Shepherds have a responsibility to keep the sheep from toxic doses of falsehood and error.

To help the flock grow, shepherds must know how to communicate the basic ingredients of spiritual growth and discipleship. Many pastors have a problem in this area. They may be great pulpiteers, but the thought of giving individual attention to a person and helping him or her grow is terrifying and mysterious. Why? Because no one ever led them through the basic steps. Much of what they learned in seminary was not geared toward helping individuals. And many pastors have left the ministry for this very reason.

I once had a couple of hours with one of the most motivated pastors I'd talked with in years. Six months prior to our chat, he was going to leave his church and go into secular work. He just did not know how to help people grow. Many were coming to Christ and they needed to grow in their faith. His sermons helped a little, but he knew they needed much more than that. He was frustrated, defeated, brokenhearted, and on the way out. But thank God he had a friend who knew how to help people grow. They talked for hours, days, weeks, months. The picture began to clear and he put what he learned to work. Today he has 12 men in his church whom he is discipling. They in turn are nearly to the point where they can begin to repeat the process in the lives of others. Helping people to begin morning prayer and Bible reading, Scripture memory, Bible study, meditating on and applying the Word to their lives, is not difficult.

But two things are musts. First, leaders must be doing these things themselves. Paul was clear about this. "Whatever you have learned or received or heard from me, or seen in me—put it into practice. And the God of peace will be with you" (Phil. 4:9).

Second, leaders must ask God for a shepherd's heart and servant's spirit. They will not maintain this sort of ministry for very long without these qualities. Leaders may enter ministry with a flurry of enthusiasm, but when the realities of spiritual pediatrics are in full bloom, they will be tempted to look for an easier pathway of service.

3. *Sloth*. Shepherding is hard work. It is a work of faith and a labor of love. Pastors labor in the Word and in doctrine. They labor fervently in prayer. In many ways it is like raising a family. Each one needs individual, personal attention and that is hard work. It is both taxing and time consuming. But it must be done.

4. *Diversions*. I have observed that when leaders commit themselves to a ministry of individual personal attention, a host of other opportunities wait in the wings to lure them off the track. Glorious opportunities! They must examine these opportunities under the light of their main job and calculate their priorities very carefully. The ministry of discipling people and meeting their needs can look rather dim in the bright light of things that are big, noisy, and accompanied by a flare of excitement. There is little glamour in the day-to-day work of caring for the welfare of people.

In a meeting of mission directors in San Diego, the phrase "glorious opportunity" became a catchword. It all began one morning, when one of the men spoke of the glorious opportunity he had had that past week to serve the Lord. He described the event in glowing terms, going on and on about his involvement in the glorious opportunity. Finally, the man who was chairing the meeting asked a pointed question.

"It all sounds quite fascinating and exciting, but what does it have to do with the mission that God has given our organization?"

A silence fell on the room as they looked at the first man, awaiting his answer. He seemed a little confused and finally he blurted out, "Well, probably nothing—but it was a glorious opportunity!"

During the rest of the week, the men chuckled from time to time about the incident. But they also thought a great deal about the implications of the question and answer.

I have been impressed that whenever Lorne Sanny gets his top leadership together, the first thing he does is to review with us the objectives of our mission. In fact, Lorne says that his primary responsibility is to help set, clarify, and maintain the objectives of our organization. I agree. And the reason, of course, is that it is so easy to be diverted into some Glorious Opportunity that appears.

There are three ways you could destroy your life. One is to do nothing with it, to give in to that lazy streak in you and just sit idle while the world and its terrible needs go weeping by. The second is to give yourself to the wrong thing; to fight and claw after something for an entire lifetime, only to discover, finally, that you have given your life to the wrong thing. The third way is through diversions. You are generally on the right track, but you periodically observe some Glorious Opportunity that leads down a bypath, and follow blindly after it.

Opportunities to Meet Needs

There is great need for Christian leaders who will take time to learn the needs of their people and then meet those needs.

Self-centeredness, ignorance, sloth, and diversion all fight against leaders who would set their hearts to feed their flock. But by God's grace, anyone can become a diligent leader who looks out for people.

During World War II, I was stationed for a time at Camp Pendleton near San Clemente, California. We used to go to Los Angeles and Hollywood when we had weekend passes. In Hollywood in those days there were men known as zoot-suiters. They wore suits with extremely long coats and baggy pants that were pegged at the ankles, gaudy wide-brimmed hats, and gold watch chains that practically dragged on the ground. One weekend a gang of them got together to have some fun beating up on marines. Fifteen or twenty of them would find a lone marine and pound him senseless. It was great fun for them, and they clobbered a half dozen marines on that weekend. The commander of our base was horrified. So the next weekend any marine that wanted to volunteer for extra duty was told to fall out in dungarees and boots. They were loaded in the back of a truck and driven to Hollywood. All weekend they drove the streets of Hollywood looking for zoot-suiters. When they found some, they hopped off the truck and dealt with them. From that weekend until the end of the war, there was no record of a marine being attacked by zoot-suiters in Hollywood. While the commander's method was questionable, it was obvious he was looking out for the welfare of his men.

One time when I was in the Denver airport on my way to Wichita, Kansas, I noticed an unusual number of airline personnel gathered at the gate where our plane was to load. A large group of boat people was about to arrive from Los Angeles.

I watched as scores of confused and hesitant people came off the plane. They were wearing badges, carrying plastic bags given by the Red Cross, and wondering where to go and what to do. However, they didn't have to wonder for long, for relief workers and airline personnel were there to meet them. Many of the relief agency people and the airline personnel probably had never heard of Solomon's advice about paying attention to the needs of the people committed to their care. But they were doing it. Some refugees were wearing badges marked "Lutheran Immigration and Refugee Service." Others were wearing large black and yellow pins with the letters U.S.C.C. Some were carrying plastic bags reading "Donated by German Red Cross Federal Republic.' One worker was especially efficient. She would note their badges, lead them to the proper gates, ask them to sit down, and then swing into action getting their boarding passes, pointing out the restrooms, and making sure they were properly informed as to when the next flights would be. All in all, the workers were terrific. Soon the refugees were smiling, relaxed, and at ease. They knew they would be cared for.

When people know someone is taking care of them, they will normally respond as these refugees did. Leaders who look out for the welfare of their people will have a group of followers who are motivated and eager to follow them.

A friend of mine once visited our home in Colorado Springs, shortly after he resigned his commission in the air force. Since Ray had been teaching at an air force leadership school for the past two years, we spent a lot of time talking about leadership and its effect on morale and motivation. During one of our conversations, he told me about his first squadron commander, Lt. Col. Billy J. Brown. He noted that Colonel Brown's most notable quality was that he took care of the people in his squadron. Because of the nature of their jobs, some of the aircrews were required to spend long periods away from home. While these crews were gone, often for three months at a time, Colonel Brown was diligent to check with each of their families weekly to see if they had any needs.

Another aspect of the squadron's mission required each aircrew to be away from home for seven days every three weeks throughout the year. During this time, the crews were restricted to a certain area of the base, and separated from their families. Frequently an aircrew member scheduled for restricted duty faced a potential problem at home—his wife expecting a child during his restricted duty, or a sick child who needed to be hospitalized. In such cases, Colonel Brown always kept in touch with these men and their families and monitored the situations closely. In addition, he always scheduled a backup crewmember to cover for these men if an emergency did arise. All of the crewmembers knew that most of the commanders on other bases refused to meet individual needs like this. Ray told me that because of this personal concern, the men in his squadron felt that Colonel Brown was deeply interested in their lives, on and off the job. Their problems were his problems. As a result, morale was high and the men were motivated to do their best for him. They didn't mind working long, hard hours or even pulling extra duty, because they knew Colonel Brown would take care of them.

By way of contrast, Ray told me about other commanders who produced the opposite effect. They didn't meet the personal needs of their people, and as a result, morale suffered. Based on his discussions with hundreds of officers during his tour as a leadership instructor, Ray concluded that the first concern of young officers in the air force today is whether their superiors are really looking out for the welfare of their people or simply taking care of themselves. He observed that on bases where commanders were going out of their way to take care of their people, morale and motivation were high. However, on bases where commanders were not doing this, resignations were high instead.

A leader must watch out for his people and tend to their needs. Solomon said, "Be sure you know the condition of your flocks, give careful attention to your herds" (Prov. 27:23). God has called us to be shepherds. Our Master's words to Peter should be enough motivation for us: "Jesus said . . . Do you truly love me? . . . Take care of my sheep'" (John 21:16).

CHAPTER SEVEN

Be a Communicating Leader

During the summer that Virginia, Randy, and I spent about a month behind the Iron Curtain, the only news we heard was from Radio Moscow. A man with a lovely British accent would give the news broadcast from Moscow. As he told of the inhumane and treacherous deeds of the U.S. Air Force in Africa, he said, "The drone of their bombers drown out the denials of their president." Week after week we were fed the Communist party line. It was depressing and disturbing.

Finally, the day came to fly from Prague, Czechoslovakia, to Geneva, Switzerland. We arrived at the hotel, went out for a bite of lunch, and then headed for the newsstand. We located *Newsweek, Time,* and the *Herald Tribune* and then returned to our room and read each of them. Because we were starved for the news of what was happening in the world, we made a daily trip to the newsstand. Like most people, we had a craving to be informed.

A Leader Informs

Whether we're talking about international events or the workings of a group of people, we all like to be informed. Leaders must be conscious of this need in the people with whom they are working.

Dawson Trotman was a master at keeping people informed. During my early years with The Navigators, all of us at the International Headquarters were instructed to keep Thursday nights open. On that evening each week, we would gather in the living room of Daws and Lila's home at Glen Eyrie, and Daws would brief us. He would read letters from the missionaries and have reports from the reps that happened to be at the Glen. He would also just share with us current blessings from the Word— what God was teaching him. Then he would bring us up to date on his current thinking, plans, ideas, and forthcoming projects. He especially enjoyed announcing engagements. He would drag out the announcement to keep us in suspense, and finally reveal the happy news.

I look back on those evenings with fond memories, for they were the highlight of the week. God used those times to keep our morale high and infuse us with a great sense of excitement and gladness. Even though my job was not all that important in those days, Daws made me feel that I was necessary—to him, to the ministry, to accomplishing the task, to the Great Commission. Yes, it took time, effort, and thought on his part to weld us into a team. We were the "Nav family," his and Lila's "Dear Gang." And we felt it.

Keeping people informed is Godlike. God could have left us in the dark about how the world came into being, but He didn't. "In the beginning God created the heavens and the earth" (Gen. 1:1).

He could have left us in ignorance about how sin entered the world, but He didn't.

> The LORD God took the man and put him into the Garden of Eden to work it and take care of it. And the LORD God commanded the man, "You are free to eat from any tree in the garden; but you must not eat from the tree of the knowledge of good and evil, for when you eat of it you will surely die" (Gen. 2:15-17).

He could have left us to speculate about the origin of the Bible. But He didn't. "All Scripture is God-breathed" (2 Tim. 3:16). "For prophecy never had its origin in the will of man, but men spoke from God as they were carried along by the Holy Spirit" (2 Peter 1:21).

We were not left to our imaginations about these things, for we might have dreamed up all sorts of theories. But God in His mercy turned on the light. He chose to reveal to us the great mysteries of the universe. Why do you suppose He did that? Because it is His nature to keep His people informed. For some reason He wants us to know. It is His way of doing things. "He made known his ways to Moses, his deeds to the people of Israel" (Ps. 103:7). The leader will do well to remember this. Any group, any organization, any board of elders or deacons, any corps of Sunday School teachers functions better if it feels it is up-to-date and "in the know."

1 once read of a professional athletic team that was losing games. Morale and motivation were low, and there was bickering and strife among the athletes. When a reporter probed into the situation, he discovered the root cause: the players did not know what the management was thinking and so they fed on rumors. Was the club going to remain in the city where they were playing or would they be moved across the country? Were the players secure in their jobs, or would they be traded? Was the owner going to fire the manager? And on and on. Nobody had answers. Just questions. Team members felt suspicious and anxious, and this affected their game. They knew they weren't playing well, and this made them mad because they knew they could do better. And their poor performance angered the coaches. And so on around the circle. Their real problem was a management problem. Their leaders were not doing their jobs.

It is interesting to note that the Apostle Paul used teams of people to dispense information.

> Tychicus will tell you all the news about me. He is a dear brother, a faithful minister and fellow servant in the Lord. I am sending him to you for the express purpose that you may know about our circumstances and that he may encourage your hearts. He is coming with Onesimus, our faithful and dear brother, who is one of you. They will tell you everything that is happening here (Col. 4:7-9).

It was important to Paul that people knew what was going on, who was going or staying where, and how different ones were getting along. Note how frequently things like this appeared in his letters: "Erastus stayed in Corinth, and I left Trophimus sick in Miletus" (2 Tim. 4:20). "Timothy, my fellow worker, sends his greetings to you, as do Lucius, Jason and Sosipater, my relatives" (Rom. 16:21). "Only Luke is with me" (2 Tim. 4:11).

What was he trying to accomplish by all of this? To help all of these people feel part of the movement? To muster prayer support? To keep them motivated? To make them feel important to the work of Christ? Probably all of these things and more. And any good leader today will do likewise.

My first independent assignment with The Navigators was to work in a student ministry in Pittsburgh. After my wife and I had moved there, we heard that The Navigators were attempting to purchase Glen Eyrie in Colorado. Humanly speaking, this was an impossibility, for we had six weeks to raise $100,000, almost half of our annual budget. It was more money than we had ever dreamed of raising. But Daws believed that he had the mind of God in the matter and mobilized the staff to action. I was new to the staff, and didn't really feel a part of the team as yet. But Daws soon changed all that. I began to get letters from him telling me how the campaign was going. I wrote frequently, sending in the money that we were able to raise. He was thankful and enthusiastic, and his spirit was catching. Soon I found myself swept along in the momentum. I knew I was having a part in a modern-day miracle.

A Fool Withholds Information

Solomon says, "The lips of the wise spread knowledge; not so the hearts of fools" (Prov. 15:7). The *Authorized Version* uses the word *disperse*, which means "to scatter or diffuse." A wise person spreads the word, while a fool does not. I have been involved in various undertakings where secrecy seemed to be the order of the day, and for the wrong reasons. In one instance, information was withheld because it made those who had it feel superior to those who didn't. It was a status symbol, and those of us who were on the outside looking in felt inferior to the group who knew things we didn't. They were the "in-group"; everybody else was a second-class citizen. This is devastating to morale and demoralizing to those who are treated in such a shabby manner. As a general rule, it is better to disperse knowledge than withhold it. That which is communicated with humility and prudence is a blessing to all that receive it. *People crave information that bears on their lives*—and the wise leader knows how to communicate it with wisdom.

Many years ago, I personally experienced the effects of withholding information from people. My wife and I were in Fiji for a ministry assignment at the University of the South Pacific in the city of Suva. We flew back to Nandi to take a plane to New Zealand where I was due to speak at a men's retreat the coming weekend. But there was a problem. The airplane workers who fueled the planes at the Auckland, New Zealand airport were on strike. Nothing was flying from Fiji to Auckland. Day after day we walked to the Nandi airport to ask about the situation, but they were unable to tell us a thing. Then one day we got a phone call. There was a Pan Am plane coming through with some seats available on a first-come, first-served basis. The next morning we were at the airport. We weren't first in line, but we were close. We checked in and were issued boarding passes. But more problems. No one was quite sure how many seats were empty. For days we had been held in suspense. No information. Now, with boarding passes in hand, we were still in suspense. Would we get on? No one knew. So we waited. We prayed. And believe it or not, even after the plane was in, no one could tell us yes or no—go or no go. It wasn't until we walked in the door of the 747 that we were certain we would be leaving. It was a strange situation—full of suspense and anxiety. The one thing we needed was information.

A Leader Continuously Informs

In the summer of 1976, when I had the privilege of speaking at the morning worship service of the Evergreen Baptist Church, I was amazed to see a 14-year-old boy reading the Scriptures, giving the announcements, and leading in prayer. The pastor was sitting beside me, and I asked him about it. He explained it was a practice he had followed for many years. That week it was the turn of the youth department to lead the service. Next week the ladies of the church would lead, the following week the men, and so on. His statement was significant: "When I leave here, they will know as much about running a church as I do." Here was a man who was dispersing knowledge among his people.

It is especially important for a leader to *brief the people at the beginning of any project*. This will help the leader find out how others feel about it. If they are enthusiastic to begin, they can then appoint a few from their group to work with the leader in formulating plans. After some time when the leader senses the backing of the people and the mind of God on the matter, he or she should call the group together and lay out the plan.

- Here is my suggestion as to what we should do next—and why I think so. What do you think?

- Here's how I feel God would have us go about it, and what we need to do to accomplish the task.

- Here are my suggestions as to people who should take responsibility for various phases of the project, and reasons why they are suggested.

- Here's what it's going to cost us in time and money.

- Here's when I hope to have the work completed.

The leader should spread the word to all that will be affected. And the leader should do everything possible to keep people informed at each phase of the endeavor.

The leader must keep in mind that people crave information, and are pleased when they are kept up to date. "Pleasant words are a honeycomb, sweet to the soul and healing to the bones" (Prov. 16:24). How many things do you know of that are both healthful and sweet? Not many. We are told from our childhood, "Don't eat that, it will make you fat. . . . Don't eat this, it will rot your teeth. . . . Don't eat that, it's not good for you."

But not so with pleasant words, for they are both sweet and healthful. When leaders apply this principle, they will discover that the people will enjoy getting the information and they will be a healthy lot—motivated, with their morale at a high peak.

Solomon offered advice about the kinds of information that are valuable.

1. *Timely information.* "A man finds joy in giving an apt reply— and how good is a timely word!" (Prov. 15:23) The timely word is a blessing—both to the giver and receiver, and the leader will find joy in sharing that which is helpful. But there is a time to speak. Quite often the leader's words are not as effective as they might

be because they are ill timed. There is "a time to be silent and a time to speak" (Ecc. 3:7). If a leader jumps the gun and shares before the people are ready, he or she errs. If a person waits too long, the rumor mill may take over. And when rumors are flying rather than truth being dispersed, the enterprise can be in big trouble.

James reminds us that the tongue can do much damage.

> Likewise the tongue is a small part of the body, but it makes great boasts. Consider what a great forest is set on fire by a small spark. The tongue also is a fire, a world of evil among the parts of the body. It corrupts the whole person, sets the whole course of his life on fire, and is itself set on fire by hell (James 3:5-6).

While the tongue can do much damage, when it used right, it disperses a blessing.

2. Accurate information. The leader is preserved by both loyalty and truth. "Loyalty and truth preserve the king; and he upholds his throne by righteousness" (Prov. 20:28, NASB). When a leader practices telling people the truth in every situation, stability and confidence develop. But if people are never sure if they are being told the truth, the whole operation becomes shaky. People will not knowingly follow a liar. Deception and falsehood are death to the leader.

A friend once told me of an incident that illustrates this point. This pastor of a church was frequently called to go to other churches to conduct evangelistic services. When he would return to his congregation, he would report the results. But there was a problem—his reports were always exaggerated. What his parishioners heard from people in the churches where the pastor had visited always differed from the pastor's reports. Some of the members of the congregation he pastored found it funny, but others found it unnerving. "If he lies to us about this," they said, "possibly he is lying to us about other things as well." They began to resent it, and soon they became convinced they should get rid of him. A vote was taken and he was fired. Followers must be able to depend on the leader's word.

3. Appropriate information. A leader can sometimes share too much information with people. There are certain things that are better kept quiet or shared with only a few. If the leader shares certain things with new Christians, it can do them spiritual damage. They may have no way to relate to the information, and could become offended. It could plant seeds of doubt or fear in their minds; if they take it wrong, they could become angry or bitter. Here again we see the importance of the leader knowing the people with whom he is working. Solomon said, "The tongue of the wise commends knowledge" (Prov. 15:2). That's the essence of the point. A leader should share what the people can accept, assimilate, and understand.

In 1958 I was running a Navigator ministry in Lincoln, Nebraska. A number of young leaders whom my wife and I were training were living in our home with us. One of them came to me and asked if one of his friends could move into the home for a couple of weeks. It was spring break at the university and he had no place to stay. I was against the idea. He was a brand-new believer and the environment of our home was pitched at a high level of Christian maturity. But Bob pressed the point. He thought it would probably do his friend a lot of good. Rather than make a big thing out of it, I finally agreed, against my better judgment.

The guy moved in, and it wasn't long before he began to resent some of the things that we were doing. Early morning prayer . . . early morning Bible study . . . conversation that was way over his head. He became sullen. In a few days he moved out. He just wasn't able to assimilate the things we did and discussed. Rather than being built up by his stay, he left very discouraged. While leaders should normally be open and share freely with people, there are some times when they must cautiously select the information they disperse to certain people.

4. Motivating information. Solomon had keen insight here. "A wise man's heart guides his mouth, and his lips promote instruction (Prov. 16:23). This is one of the most powerful verses in the entire Bible on the subject of motivation. When the heart motivates a leader's words, they are persuasive. When the leader merely quotes General So-and-so, or Doctor Somebody, the words do not have the same punch as saying, "Here is a truth that I have experienced in my life," and then sharing from the heart.

All of us can tell the great difference between a person who merely speaks what he has read or heard and one who shares what he has felt and tasted. The timely truth that is dispersed must come from the heart. There must be conviction undergirding the knowledge that is shared. The heart is the best communicator. When the heart is teaching the lips of the leader, it adds persuasiveness to his speech. There is conviction, life, warmth, and sincerity—what is commonly termed *heart*.

Communication takes thought, effort, and planning. But it is well worth it.

CHAPTER EIGHT

Be a Goal Oriented Leader

Never in her entire life had the lady shared her faith in Jesus Christ with anyone. She was approaching middle age and had a burning desire to witness. But the whole thing seemed a bit out of reach. She was living a fine Christian life, but she simply did not know how to start, what to say, or how to go about it.

Our group had been invited to conduct a witnessing seminar at her church. When this lady learned of the seminar, she was ecstatic. She had prayed for years that she would be able to get some practical help in becoming an effective witness for Christ. Maybe this would be the answer to her prayers.

On the night when the seminar began, a rather large crowd assembled. There was an excitement in the air. We had been holding these seminars every week all summer in the Washington, D.C. area, and this was the largest group of the summer.

So we began. The plan was simple. I gave a brief description of the two-night curriculum and then shared a few passages from the Scriptures on the importance of witnessing. I told them our overall goal was to teach them how to tell others how to establish a relationship with Jesus Christ and that we would teach them step by step how to do this. Our first night was spent teaching the people how to give their testimonies. Since most had never done this, we went slowly, simply, and methodically through the Scriptures about the subject. Our key passage was Acts 26, which records Paul's personal testimony before King Agrippa.

We broke the class into small groups and our team went to work. One member of the team helped each person formulate the salient facts regarding his or her conversion experience and Christian growth. The lady had a rather ordinary yet powerful story. After she thought it through, a team member helped her write it out. She entered into the spirit of it with great enthusiasm.

Then we dropped the bombshell. Their homework assignment was to go to a friend, a neighbor, or a relative and tell that person the story. Although some were a bit nervous, the assignment didn't seem to shake this lady at all. She had waited for years for help like this, and she was eager to get her toes in the water.

We reassembled the groups, sang a hymn, had prayer, and dismissed. It was around 9:00 P.M. As the lady left, she thought to herself, *Why should I wait until tomorrow? My boss is working late. Why not go to the office and see if he will listen to my story?*

So she caught a downtown bus, went up the elevator to the office, and, sure enough, there he was. He looked up, surprised to see her.

She told him that she was involved in a seminar and that part of her assignment was to give her testimony to someone before the second session the next evening. She asked if he would like to hear her story.

"Sure," he said. "I'll get some coffee and take a break and listen." So she began. She told him what her life had been like before she had accepted Christ. Then she told him of the circumstances surrounding her conversion and what the Lord had done in her life since that time.

As she finished her story, the man turned pale. Visibly shaken, he said, "What I have heard tonight must be why I was spared." And he told her this story.

Some years before he had been invited to a cocktail party, and on the way he had had not one, but three flat tires and had missed the party completely. Most of the people at the party had died of food poisoning. He knew God had spared his life.

Now here was this friend telling him this marvelous story of her salvation in Christ.

"That's wonderful," he said. "But how can I experience this?"

"Oh," she said, "we haven't learned that part yet. That comes tomorrow night when we learn to share the bridge illustration. You'll have to wait until then."

The next night we began our second seminar by asking the students to share with the rest of the group what had happened when they gave their testimonies. The lady stood and told us the story. I had never seen a person so motivated to learn how to explain the Redemption Story. She took careful notes, got it all clearly in mind, and when the seminar ended, headed back downtown to tell her boss the rest of the story. She was well on her way to becoming an effective witness for Christ. She had been shown a goal that was attainable. It was a simple thing—well within her reach. We helped her attain the goal; and as a result, she happily moved ahead in witnessing.

There is an important principle embedded in this little story. People need goals and they also need help reaching them. Often the situation calls for them to set their own goals and a timetable to reach them. On occasion—as in a classroom situation—they have the goals and timetable set for them. But in either case, people need goals at a level where they can reach them. Good leadership does what it can to help people set these goals, monitor their progress, and keep moving ahead on time, on track, and on target.

Setting Goals

Goal setting is a foreign idea to vast numbers of people. So leaders often must move very slowly as they introduce the concept to the people with whom they are involved. Why do people need goals? Three reasons come immediately to mind.

1. Direction. People need goals to provide direction for their lives. It is impossible for people to press toward the mark if there is no mark. It is impossible for them to finish their course if there is no finish line.

Let's say the State of Colorado is sponsoring a mountain-climbing contest. Thirty competitors show up in Boulder to take part in the big event. They gather together and the sponsor of the event arrives, to give them instructions. All he has in his hand is a starting gun. "Okay," he says. "Go!"

"Go? Where? Which peak? Longs Peak? Pikes Peak?"

The room is filled with loud complaints. No one knows where to go or what to do. Even though they may be the top thirty mountain climbers in the nation, they are immobilized if they don't know which mountain to climb. They can't function. The people of God need goals to provide direction.

2. Progress. Goals are important to ensure progress. Without them, the people can be like rocking chairs, with movement but no progress. An absence of goals can endanger the life of the church. The church machinery may function in a whirl of activities— committee meetings, ladies' circles, and the like—but if there is no primary goal toward which the body of believers is striving, the program may be feverish but going nowhere.

3. Accomplishment. The third reason for goals is to accomplish a purpose. He who shoots at nothing hits it. If I have no goal, I will never know when I am finished. I can work day and night for weeks, months, and years; but without a specific goal I will never complete the task. Why? Because there is no task. I have not set out to do anything measurable. Therefore, I never get anything measurable done.

Even though these are good reasons to set goals, some people feel the whole notion of establishing goals is unspiritual. Somehow it sounds like work done in the energy of the flesh. "And we all know where that leads and how much such can accomplish for the glory of God!"

Goals and Scripture

However, as we look into the Scriptures, we do find evidence of well-thought-out plans and objectives. In 1953 I moved to Pittsburgh to launch a campus ministry. It was my first assignment and I needed direction. One of the passages the Lord gave me was 1 Corinthians 2:1-5:

> When I came to you, brothers, I did not come with eloquence or superior wisdom as I proclaimed to you the testimony about God. For I resolved to know nothing while I was with you except Jesus Christ and Him crucified. I came to you in weakness and fear, and with much trembling. My message and

my preaching were not with wise and persuasive words, but with a demonstration of the Spirit's power, so that your faith might not rest on men's wisdom, but on God's power.

In the margin of my Bible I wrote, "Claimed for ministry in Pittsburgh, June 25, 1953."

As we look at that passage, we note that Paul had a predetermined plan that he had carefully thought through. He also had a practical goal in mind. His plan: to preach Christ crucified. His goal: that the faith of the Corinthian Christians should rest on the power of God.

One of Nehemiah's objectives in building the wall was that they might "no longer be in disgrace" (Neh. 2:17). Solomon said in his prayer of dedication of the temple,

> Then hear from heaven, your dwelling place, and do whatever the foreigner asks of you, so that all the peoples of the earth may know your name and fear you, as do your own people Israel, and may know that this house I have built bears your Name" (1 Kings 8:43).

Christians should most assuredly ask the Lord for specific guidance about specific plans that move toward specific goals. Paul pressed toward the mark. He said, "But one thing I do" (Phil. 3:13). He had a goal.

Long-Range Goals

Leaders should help their people first focus on their long-range objectives. For unless people have evaluated their overall life goals, they have no basis for determining more immediate, everyday goals. That, of course, is the problem in the lives of most Christians. Like their unsaved neighbors, they may have certain long-range goals for which they are striving in the everyday affairs of life. They may have set goals in the area of financial security, physical health, a happy family life, and so on. But it never occurs to most believers that they must set certain long-range goals for themselves spiritually, if they are to accomplish anything for the Lord, or become the people God wants them to be.

Goals can vary; but unless people have long-range goals burning in their hearts, they will have no basis for setting their spiritual activities on a daily basis. Their long-range goals determine their short-range goals.

Short-Range Goals

Once people have determined their long-range goals, the leader should help them determine the short-range goals, which will help them meet their objectives.

A track star had to learn to take her first step, like any other child. When she was learning to walk, her parents held out their hands and encouraged their child to venture forth on that awesome first step. And then the magic moment came when she let go of every-thing and took that first unaided step. The parents stayed close with smiles, assurances, and urgings. They were only a step away. It would have been foolish for them to have tried to make the child walk the length of the room. That came later. For soon she was walking by herself, and then running, jumping, and skipping. And finally, under the supervision of a track coach, she prepared for the Olympic games.

Short-range goals are essential in accomplishing long-range goals. For instance, let's say the leader has a new Christian in the fellow-ship whose primary goal is to become a man of God. What will the leader do? Encourage a great leap forward? No, the leader will suggest things on a short-range basis that are in direct line with the new Christian's long-range goal. For instance, the leader might suggest the practice of morning prayer and Bible reading. Why? Because those things are in direct line with the objective. So are Bible study, church membership, Scripture memorization, and meditation on the Word. One of the leader's jobs is to help people select realistic goals for themselves; and usually this means toning down overambitious goals that would prove too difficult to reach.

When I was working as a representative of The Navigators in the Midwest, I often made trips to Oklahoma State University. One of the new converts I met was Carl McCutchan. Carl was a new babe in Christ and eager to grow. Joe Lee Holt, the man who had won

Carl to Christ, had suggested that Carl read the New Testament. So Carl began. He became so engrossed in the New Testament that he began to neglect his university studies. He read through the New Testament again and again—eight to ten times a week. He couldn't put it down. His grades began to drop, and he almost flunked out of school. When we found out what was happening, we had to go to Carl and help him strike a balance. We didn't want to cool his ardor for Christ, but neither did we want him to flunk out of school. So we helped him set some attainable goals that helped him remain in college and grow spiritually as well.

One winter our family went to Steamboat Springs for a few days of skiing. Randy took his camera along to get some pictures of some of the activities on the slopes. We got shots of him doing various daredevil jumps—exciting maneuvers called the Back Scratcher, Tip Drop, Mule Kick, and Helicopter.

As I looked at the pictures, I was reminded of his first few times on the slopes when Mark Sulcer took him and a few of his buddies and taught them the basics: how to snowplow on the bunny slopes, how to turn, how to parallel, and so on. Very easy, very slow and simple stuff. But those things were necessary to his becoming the sort of skier who could speed down any slope on the mountain. These were easily attainable short-range goals that were in direct line with his long-range goal—to become an expert skier.

Short-range goals are necessary for motivation and morale. Solomon said, "A longing fulfilled is sweet to the soul" (Prov. 13:19). Breaking a project down into small, bite-sized units that are reachable keeps people going. Frankly, that is why I usually suggest that people begin a study of the New Testament by studying a few of the shorter books. At a chapter a week, it takes only three weeks to complete the Book of Titus, four weeks for Colossians, five weeks for 1 John, and so on. Once people have actually completed a study of a few of the New Testament books, they can then launch out on one of the longer ones. But if they start with Matthew, it is 28 weeks before they have studied even one book. However, if after only three weeks there is that "desire accomplished" of having actually studied a whole book of the

Bible, people will most likely be motivated by accomplishing their goal. After some years they will have studied the entire New Testament; but to begin, they need that incentive of a desire accomplished. "Hope deferred makes the heart sick, but a longing fulfilled is a tree of life" (Prov. 13:12). Delay can mean discouragement. It is important to help people attain some goals, to give them the sense of accomplishment, and help them gain momentum.

People need help in determining God's goals for them, and then in making God's goals their goals. Solomon said that desire accomplished is sweet to the soul. However, not all desire accomplished is sweet to the soul. Note Psalm 106:15: "So He gave them what they asked for, but sent a wasting disease upon them." A parallel passage to this is Ecclesiastes 2:10-11:

> I denied myself nothing my eyes desired; I refused my heart no pleasure. My heart took delight in all my work, and this was the reward for all my labor. Yet when I surveyed all that my hands had done and what I had toiled to achieve, everything was meaningless, a chasing after the wind; nothing was gained under the sun.

From these passages we can see that satisfaction comes in achieving those things that God lays on our heart. Fleshly desire accomplished is void of satisfaction. It is hollow, filled with disappointment. But, the fulfillment of something that God has impressed on our spirits is indeed sweet to the soul.

Goals and Fulfillments

Solomon suggested how to ensure that goals will result in a sense of fulfillment and satisfaction. He said, "Commit to the LORD whatever you do, and your plans will succeed" (Prov. 16:3).

Leaders must teach their followers to actively seek the will of God and to base their plans on God's will. Solomon no doubt learned this from his father David, who said, "Commit your way to the LORD; trust in him and he will do this" (Ps. 37:5).

There are two reasons for committing plans and programs to the

Lord. First, all of our plans are to be for the glory of God. He must give the plan and receive the glory when it is accomplished. Second, our plans are too heavy for us to bear alone. In fact, the word commit literally means "roll them upon Him, as a burden too heavy to be born by yourself."

To proceed with God-given plans in faith, humility, and total dependence on Him, with an eye to His glory alone, is the sure path to success. God has given us the responsibility of planning. "To man belong the plans of the heart" (Prov. 16:1). The word plans suggests the idea of placing things in proper order. We see the same word picture in the story of Abraham who "built an altar there and arranged the wood" (Gen. 22:9). God gave us a brain and He expects us to use it. Planning and organizing—placing things in proper order—are responsibilities placed squarely on the shoulders of those who serve God. Good leaders will teach their followers how to do these things.

Goals and Persistence

Teaching people to determine God's goals for themselves, and to stick to those goals, is not always an easy task for a leader. It is all too easy for followers to be swayed by others, letting others influence their goals. The Apostle Paul warned, "Each one should test his own actions. Then he can take pride in himself, without comparing himself to somebody else" (Gal. 6:4). Paul pictured a man who looked back at this life and felt good about what he saw. He had not been motivated by unhealthy comparison with another person.

It is difficult, however, to keep from letting others influence our thinking, and to listen to God alone.

Some time ago, a friend of mine talked with a group of seminary students about the basics of the Christian life. As they talked, these men expressed that their biggest sense of defeat during their years in seminary stemmed from their failure to consistently maintain a program of morning prayer and Bible reading and personal Bible study. As my friend talked with them further, he found that as they were caught up in the academic system at their school, they began to compete for better grades in their courses. When they looked around at other students and saw them getting better grades, they began to spend more time studying to improve their grades. Soon they found their lives so absorbed in academics that they no longer had time to meet God personally every day. While these men knew a personal relationship with God should be the number-one priority in their lives, they had altered their goals and made their number-one priority achieving good grades. Comparing themselves with their peers sidetracked them from one of God's goals for them.

Paul's words apply: "So then, each of us will give an account of himself to God" (Rom. 14:12). Since we are accountable to God, our goals should come from Him.

Leaders must help their people keep this perspective. They can help people set reasonable and attainable goals. However, they must not try to cram their ideas and standards down others' throats. They need to let God speak to others, and let God show people what is right at their present level of growth and commitment. Then when people achieve the goals they set, they can rejoice and thank the Lord. If they do not achieve them, they can go to the Lord and ask for His continued forgiveness and strength. They are responsible to God in the matter.

Goals and Action

Leaders' responsibilities don't end after they have helped their followers set long-range and short-range goals. Next they must show their followers how to put those goals into action.

1. Timing. It is important to teach people when to act. It is equally as dangerous to dart ahead too quickly as it is to lag behind. When to do something is of equal weight and consequence as what to do. I was once discussing this very thing with the president of an international Christian mission. He had gotten a letter from a director in the field that told of a plan they were contemplating. They had their goals carefully set and were seeking his advice. They were eager to get underway and asked that the president read their letter and then give them a telephone call, hopefully to give them the green light to move ahead. As we discussed the matter, the president said, "I think they are on the right track, but their timing is off. They are about a year ahead of themselves. My advice to them is going to be to wait."

The importance of proper timing cannot be overstated. Even though people feel a strong urge to plunge ahead, they must be taught to temper their emotions with wisdom and discretion.

2. Implementation. Leaders must make sure their people know how to implement the goals they have set for themselves. To know what to do and when to do it, but not to know how to do it breeds frustration. I was discipling a young potential laborer years ago, and we were confronted by this problem. He had struggled for months about resigning from the air force. I sat with him night after night in his barracks as we discussed the pros and cons. The decision seemed to shift back and forth. One night it would look like the obvious thing to do was stay in the air force. The next night, it would seem better to resign. Back and forth it went.

Finally, after months of prayer and discussion, he determined it was the will of God for him to separate from the air force. His goal was to serve the Lord as a missionary overseas. He planned to leave the service and pursue that goal. But then we faced the next problem. What should his timetable be for all of this? When should he leave the air force? So again we prayed and discussed it night after night, sitting on his bunk in the barracks. After some months the fog lifted, and he saw the answer clearly. He would get out the following summer and go to college in the fall. But where? There was a school in Nebraska he could attend. And there was one in his home state of Illinois. But the more we talked about it, the more he seemed to feel he should attend a college on the West Coast. I made a few telephone calls to a friend of mine who lived in Los Angeles, and my friend was able to help him work out the details of housing and employment. It seemed that the goal was set, the timing was decided, and all was well. But then the whole process hit a snag. His girlfriend in Illinois was against the idea, and he began to waver. So I encouraged him to commit that matter to God in prayer; the Lord worked out the situation beautifully.

And I learned that it was not enough to help this young man set his goals and establish a timetable—I also was responsible to help him diligently pursue the goals he had set.

CHAPTER NINE

Be a Decisive Leader

In the fall of 1951 our family moved to Seattle, where The Navigators were providing counselor training and follow-up for a Billy Graham Crusade. I was assigned to work in the counseling room, which meant that I set up chairs and placed counseling materials beside them, made sure the chairs were dusted clean each night, ran errands, and so on. Those were exciting days—I was a fairly new Christian and it was a thrill to see the people stream forward each night when Dr. Graham gave the invitation.

Each night after the meeting was over, part of the small Navigator team took the decision cards and went to work. They sent each person a letter of encouragement. Pastors, whose congregations were near the homes of these people, were notified. The team worked long into the night, night after night. After several days the guys and gals began to get a bit weary. One night after a particularly large response, the gang was working into the early hours of the morning. They had been at it for many hours, when one of the night watchmen stopped by. He was the friendly type. "How's the crusade going?" he asked.

One young Navigator looked up through bloodshot eyes and answered hoarsely, "Oh, the meetings are going great. But these decisions are killing me."

What he meant, of course, was that it was a lot of work to get those letters out that same night to all of those who had responded to the invitation to receive Christ into their lives. But those of us who heard the story applied it in another way as well. The phrase became a catchword among the staff. Whenever we were faced with a particularly difficult decision as to which plan to follow or what route to take in the area ministry, we would be reminded of the truth of that phrase. It was not the ministry itself that was difficult. In fact, we all loved the opportunity to be

involved in the work of evangelism and helping new converts
grow. But when difficult decisions came along, we responded the
way the follow-up worker responded to the question of the night
watchman. "The ministry is going great. But these decisions are
killing me."

Decisions Are Difficult

Many leaders feel the same way. They love the ministry, but the
decisions they must make are often the most difficult aspect of
their work. I once received a letter from a man responsible for a
large missionary program. Since the country where he was serving
was not likely to renew his visa, he must decide whom to recommend to take his place as the leader of the ministry.

A chaplain in the armed forces received an invitation from a
church to be its pastor. Should he stay in the military or leave?

A pilot in the air force was on the phone with me a number of
times telling me of his dilemma. Because of his outstanding
soul-winning ministry among his fellow officers, many felt he
should leave the air force and go to seminary. They felt he would
be an outstanding Christian leader and could profit immensely
from seminary training.

Why is decision-making such a difficult thing? I sat down with
my family and asked them if they ever had difficulty making
decisions. They said, "Yes." So I asked them what made this so
difficult. Here's a list of things they mentioned:

1. *Confusion about the will of God.* Often it takes many weeks,
    months, or years to discover God's will on a particular issue.

2. *The desire to hurt no one.* Some decisions carry with them con-
    sequences that affect the lives of many people. You may dis-
    like the idea of bringing discomfort to anyone else.

3. *A distaste for unpopularity.* This can affect everything, from
    what clothes you wear to whether or not to witness. Some
    decisions bring unfavorable reactions.

When they finished, I decided to add a few things to that list.

4. *Too busy.* You have no time to think the matter through.

5. *Cowardice.* You are simply afraid to step out and decide.

6. *Ignorance.* You don't have all the facts you need to make the decision.

7. *Pride.* If you are consumed with pride, you will not be a straight thinker. Your mind will not reveal the best plan but the plan that will bring the most glory to you. Making the right decision is often difficult, but the right decision is an imperative. One wrong turn on a drive from Minneapolis to Dallas could result in your missing the entire state of Texas! You could end up in New Orleans or Los Angeles. So it is in decision making. A wrong decision can send you down a road that leads to destruction. Decision-making is an art that you as a leader must master. Nothing lowers the morale of people more than to follow a person who consistently leads them down wrong paths.

How Do You Make Good Decisions?

How can you ensure that you will make good decisions? Some of the basic elements in decision making emerge from the Scriptures. Solomon said, "There is a way that seems right to a man, but in the end it leads to death" (Prov. 16:25).

1. *Recognize bad decisions.* It's important to realize that, as a human being, you are prone to making bad decisions. Jesus spoke of this: "They will put you out of the synagogue; in fact, a time is coming when anyone who kills you will think he is offering a service to God" (John 16:2). Paul admitted to the same problem. "I too was convinced that I ought to do all that was possible to oppose the name of Jesus of Nazareth" (Acts 26:9).

It is easy to settle for what "seems" right and walk in self-delusion. For that reason Solomon warned, "He who trusts in himself is a fool" (Prov. 28:26). The Prophet Jeremiah described the human heart as deceitful (Jer. 17:9). Who among us would repeatedly place our trust in one that constantly lies and deceives? Yet that is what many do. Leaders must not permit themselves to fall into this trap. Since we have within us the potential for every sin, every wrong decision, every foolish act, every bad judgment, every false step taken since the dawn of history, it behooves leaders to look outside themselves when making decisions.

It was a bad decision that led Eve to follow the advice of the Devil. It was a bad decision that led Aaron to make a golden calf. It was a bad decision that led David, the man after God's own heart, to wallow in the slime of immorality, murder, and deceit. It was a bad decision that led Solomon to worship false gods and become involved with strange women. The nature of mankind is to make bad decisions. This can apply to the simplest of things.

In the spring of 1977 I was asked to be the speaker at a Navigator weekend collegiate conference in Indiana. When I arrived, I was met by a couple of staff members who told me that many more collegians came than they had anticipated. For that reason, all the bedrooms were full. They had reserved a bunk for me in a room with three of the staff. Without thinking or asking questions, I said, "That will be fine."

What I didn't realize was that the room was barely big enough for one person. Also, I did not know that we were located right beside the hallway door—which squeaked and banged. And I didn't realize that the other three guys in the room snored very loudly. In fact, among the Indiana Navigators, they were known as the Chain Saw Gang.

I had arrived a bit tired, so Saturday night 1 retired early.

About 11:30 or 12:00 they came in and went to bed. Each of them began to snore. A variety of sounds—rolling thunder, wet dribble, whistles, deep throaty noises—woke me up and kept me awake. After trying to sleep through it all, I finally took my blanket and went out into the dining room where there was a plastic davenport up against the wall. I lay down on it around 4:00 A.M. and had just gotten to sleep when the cooks came in at 5:00. I made a bad decision. As I look back on it, I realize I could have saved myself a lot of trouble by asking a few questions, assessing the situation, and making a more sensible decision.

2. *Define the problem.* To make good decisions, you must ask yourself, "What's the real issue here? What's the real problem we're trying to solve?" My need at the conference was sleep. I assumed that if they provided a room, I could get some sleep. But that wasn't the case. A simple question such as, "Will it be quiet enough to get some sleep?" would have shed the light I needed to make a good decision. There was a small, inexpensive motel just down the road that would have been available and given me what I needed. My decision seemed right. But it wasn't.

The words of Paul ring clear: "Be very careful, then, how you live—not as unwise but as wise" (Eph. 5:15). Paul suggested that we are to look at all sides. That's the admonition that the leader must heed—look at all sides of the problem—study the issues and assess the situation, before the decision is made. To adequately assess the issues, leaders must try to get all the facts, an abundance of accurate information.

3. *Listen before answering.* Even if you think you already know what to do, it is wise to probe for more light. "He who answers before listening—that is his folly and his shame" (Prov. 18:13). The best way for a leader to deal with an issue is to first listen to all the facts.

I was once at a meeting of the International Leadership Team of The Navigators. As we met day by day, we discussed a wide variety of important issues that affect the ministry. One day we spent many hours discussing the many facets of a particularly knotty problem. At the end of the day, Lorne Sanny thanked us for a good day of hard work. He then said, "When I came into the meeting this morning, I had what I thought to be a solution to the problem. But thanks to you, men, I now have a great deal of added light, and I can see the issues in clearer perspective. I'm sure we are now on a better course." He did not answer until he took the time to listen.

Often leaders fail at this point. They don't want to listen to something with which they disagree. Pride enters in and they believe they know what is best.

Job's friends failed at this point. Job, on the other hand, took the time to investigate the case which he did not know. Potiphar failed to get the facts when his wife lied to him regarding Joseph (Gen. 39:17-20). The law of God forbade the folly of answering a matter before the facts are known (Deut. 13:12-14).

4. *Offer suggestions to brainstorm.* After you have satisfied yourself that you know the real issues, you are ready to take the next step in decision making. Now that you have isolated the real problem, you should gather your advisers and let them offer whatever they feel to be the best solution to the problem.

Solomon stated it precisely. "Plans fail for lack of counsel, but with many advisers they succeed" (Prov. 15:22). Leaders must provide a permissive atmosphere so that people feel they have the liberty to offer whatever they think might work. Leaders should let people brainstorm.

If leaders are fortunate enough to have people around who will offer suggestions, they are blessed indeed. Those who are wise realize they are limited in their understanding. They know they need help. Many minds applied to a problem will in all likelihood see more facets than if just one person wrestles with it. And as they talk, more ideas will come. It is interesting to note that the word consultation means generally the same as the Hebrew word *sod*, which refers to the tackle of a ship used in its steering and handling. Counsel provides direction for leaders. Any enterprise needs a great deal of guidance and advice to ensure proper direction. The whole picture here is that of leaders giving deference and paying close attention to the godly counsel of their advisers. During consultation, the group should look for various paths, for a number of solutions. They should focus on alternatives.

There are many advantages to this exercise, even in the simple matters of everyday life. Let's say the old automobile has finally come to the point where it needs to be replaced. And let's say there is a teenage son in the family who has recently gotten his driver's license. The dad wants a medium-sized, four-door—pure vanilla. The son thinks a hot sports car would be the thing to get. What will the dad do? Tell his son to be quiet? Tell him his idea is stupid? No. If he's smart, he will spend a few weekends with his son visiting the car dealers, talking it over, looking at all the angles—family trips, vacations, grocery shopping, insurance costs, the whole lot. In all likelihood they will both adjust a bit and come to a decision that suits the entire family.

There are several advantages to bringing in others to talk over a decision. First, there will be greater cooperation in carrying out the decision if the people know they had a hand in the decision process. Another is enlightenment. Obviously, greater light and more facts will be brought to bear if more than one person is involved. Also, the leaders will spot their creative thinkers and those who think conceptually. This will be of great value when they are looking for future leaders to train.

During this time the leaders will do well to keep their thoughts to themselves. If they say what they think, it might stifle discussion. Leaders should just sit there intelligently ignorant, take it all in, gain what light they can, and let the people talk. Solomon said, "There is a time for everything . . . a time to be silent and a time to speak" (Ecc. 3:1, 7). He reminds us, the wise heart knows "the proper time and procedure" (Ecc. 8:5).

5. *Narrow the field*. After a number of solutions have been offered, it is wise for you to arrange some sort of a "balance sheet." Try to think through all the possible consequences of the solutions offered. This will narrow the field somewhat.

In looking at all the possible solutions, leaders must guard against the adviser who thinks he knows it all and wonders why the leaders don't take immediate action. This is often the guy who has answers, and who wonders, "Why make a federal case out of this? We did it this way in the '70s—why not now?" He fails to realize what worked in the '70s might not be right for the present. Leaders must take time to consider all the alternatives suggested by their advisers.

6. *Wait on God*. When this is done, it is time for you to take the next step—waiting on God. Pray, committing the whole matter to the Lord. "Commit to the LORD whatever you do, and your plans will succeed" (Prov. 16:3). The vital energizing union of faith and prayer will enable you to establish your thoughts in the will of

God. The glory of God must be at the core. But waiting on God is not easy.

Yes, it is important that leaders sort out the real issue. And it is important that they receive counsel and look for the best solutions and alternate routes. But it is imperative that leaders wait on God. And here is the great failing. In my conversations with people in leadership positions around the world, this is the area where most have the greatest struggle.

They travel to work amid the noise of traffic—bus, train, automobile. At work they are surrounded by the sounds of phones, clacking keyboards, chat between cubicles, whatever. And so it goes throughout the day. To be still before God is difficult. There are always places to go, people to see, and things to be done. But in spite of all this, leaders must pull back into a private place and wait on God.

The Prophet Isaiah said it well: "Those who hope in the LORD will renew their strength. They will soar on wings like eagles; they will run and not grow weary, they will walk and not be faint" (Isa. 40:31). We certainly see this in the lives of the prophets, apostles, and in our Lord Jesus Himself.

Naturally, the work must go on and often leaders must be occupied with other things. But they must spend some time each day alone before God. King David put it forcefully: "Wait for the LORD; be strong and take heart and wait for the LORD" (Ps. 27:14). This attitude of faith and dependence is a great antidote to anxiety and a fretful spirit. Leaders who spend much time with God move ahead with the confidence that the Lord will establish their thoughts and lead them to the right decision.

7. *Make the decision.* When it is time for you to decide, make the decision. Solomon notes, "In his heart a man plans his course, but the LORD determines his steps" (Prov. 16:9).

God has given us minds and He expects us to use them. He has given us the power of choice. We must think, pray, gather information, and do all that we can to discover the real problem and assess the situation clearly. However, while we do this, we must remember in the final analysis, it is the Lord who directs. "Many are the plans in a man's heart, but it is the LORD'S purpose that prevails" (Prov. 19:21). David wrote, "But the plans of the LORD stand firm forever, the purposes of His heart through all generations" (Ps. 33:11). And the Lord said through the Prophet Isaiah,

> Remember the former things, those of long ago; I am God, and there is no other; I am God, and there is none like me. I make known the end from the beginning, from ancient times, what is still to come. I say: "My purpose will stand, and I will do all that I please." (Isa. 46:9-10).

It is truly a mystery how God accomplishes His eternally ordained purposes through people to whom He has given mind, will, and responsibility. We are not puppets. We have a free will to make our own decisions. Yet God is in charge and moves all things toward His purposes. Good decisions are a team effort that employ our free will and God's sovereignty. We have to wisely plan our way; but in doing this, we need to rely on God's direction.

Leaders will gain the confidence and respect of their people with this mark of prudence. If people see that leaders understand their job and are conscientious, they will follow gladly. When wisdom is the hallmark of a leader's speech and actions, others will join in to accomplish the task.

But they also need to see displayed a total trust in God. Leaders should not be caught leaning on their own understanding.

8. *Follow through.* The last thing left is for you to implement the solution. Again this is a team effort.

Paul reminded us, "I can do everything through him who gives me strength" (Phil. 4:13). "I can" expresses the human element of proceeding with discretion and wisdom. "Through Christ" expresses total dependence on God in faith.

Included in the immediate follow-through are these matters: What needs to be done immediately? Who is the best person to fill the job? When does it need to be accomplished? What will it cost?

High morale and enthusiasm in the ranks accompany the leader who is diligent to lead the people down the right paths, in constructive and productive service for their Lord. No one feels comfortable following a person who continually makes wrong decisions. An effective leader knows how to make good decisions.

CHAPTER TEN

Be a Competent Leader

Let's suppose you are a member of a football team. Suddenly, the coach becomes ill and resigns. You have some important games coming up, and you and the other players wonder what is going to happen to the team. Then one morning the sponsor of the team gets the players together and informs you that he has located a coach. Soon you meet the coach and begin your practice sessions.

The coach has many admirable qualities. He shows personal concern and interest in the players and their families. He is generous, gracious, and gregarious. He has a cheerful attitude, a pleasant smile, and really seems to enjoy being with the team. He works hard, is always on time, is available to the players, and gives himself unreservedly to the team. He laughs and jokes a lot, and keeps everyone in good spirits. Simply stated, he is an all-around good guy. But it soon becomes evident he has one glaring fault—he doesn't know anything about football. And that fact overshadows all the rest. He can't do the job!

Some years ago I watched this happen in an organization. One of the men near the top was promoted and a new man was appointed to take his place. At first, everyone liked him. He had all the qualities of a good Boy Scout—he was trustworthy, loyal, helpful, friendly, courteous, kind, obedient, cheerful, thrifty, brave, clean, and reverent. Everyone settled in for a future of great productivity and success.

But it soon became evident that he was just not capable of leading his department. He didn't know the job. Most of the people in the department knew more than their boss. As a result people began to grumble. The department was going nowhere. All of their great plans began to fade in the dense fog of the man's inability to do the job. The people were totally demoralized and everything soon ground to a halt. The man had to be replaced.

That he exhibited many sterling qualities, upright moral character, and great likability meant nothing anymore. Since he didn't know how to do his job, he was worthless to the enterprise.

Leaders must lead. And to lead, they must know their job. Admittedly, a leader can fake it for a time, but sooner or later it all catches up with him or her. When the people with whom the leader is involved begin to realize they are being led by a person who is unqualified and incompetent, they either leave, grumble and gripe, or force the person to leave. A leader's competence will help to make or break morale and motivation. Leaders must know their job.

Solomon spoke to this. "The wisdom of the prudent is to give thought to their ways, but the folly of fools is deception" (Prov. 14:8). He was referring to the practical sense that can apply knowledge and experience to the job at hand. Prudent people understand what's involved, how to get from A to B, how to make the enterprise produce. And notice also that it is "their way" that they understand. Leaders know their jobs. They know what it is that God wants them to do, and they stick with that.

Temptations for Leaders

Our Sunday School teacher once referred us to Hebrews 12:1. "Therefore, since we are surrounded by such a great cloud of witnesses, let us throw off everything that hinders and the sin that so easily entangles, and let us run with perseverance the race marked out for us." As he expounded on this verse, I was struck by the words *the race marked out for us*. Each of us has a race to run. Each of us has a job to do. Since it is obvious that we cannot do everything, it is then equally obvious that we must do what God gives us to do and leave the rest to someone else. That is not an easy thing to do. Our adversary often attacks us at this very point. And we as leaders are especially vulnerable. These attacks take several forms.

1. *Envy.* When the leader has contact with someone who does many things better, he or she may envy the other person's talent. I fell into this trap on my first assignment with The Navigators. My

wife and I were living in Pittsburgh, near the Rev. Ken Smith. Ken could sing like a lark. He had a vocabulary that was quite a contrast to my small town manner of speech. I tried to become like Ken, but it didn't work.

Many years later I was working alongside George Sanchez. George can also sing like a lark. He is a great song leader and master of ceremonies. When we would go on retreats, George could kick the football farther than I could. Fortunately, over the years I learned how to handle this sort of thing. I simply determined that I would stay with what God had given me to do and use the gifts God had given me. I learned to live and minister within my limits.

2. *Pride.* If the leader is gifted along a particular line, and does certain things well, he or she is tempted to hold in contempt those who are less gifted in that area. Some years ago the Lord gave me a verse that bore directly on this matter. The Apostle Paul admonished the Corinthians that they were not to be arrogant with one another. "For who makes you different from anyone else? What do you have that you did not receive? And if you did receive it, why do you boast as though you did not?" (1 Cor. 4:7). When leaders understand this principle, they are less likely to fall into the temptation of pride.

3. *Guilt.* In fellowship with other Christian leaders, a leader observes others doing excellent works that are outside of his or her own calling from God. And this comparison can bring a sense of guilt.

Recently, my wife read an article on Mother Teresa of India. After reading it she came into the study and began to lament her own shallow dedication, compared with Mother Teresa's. The article had thrown her into a tailspin. After she talked for awhile, we looked at 2 Corinthians 10:12: "We do not dare to classify or compare ourselves with some who commend themselves. When they measure themselves by themselves and compare themselves with themselves, they are not wise." This passage speaks directly to the problem. When we compare ourselves among ourselves, we can go into defeat. We must simply measure ourselves against the path that God has chosen for us.

Everybody cannot be Mother Teresa. In fact, only one person can—Mother Teresa herself. Virginia cannot care for the starving people of India, but she can lead a Bible study for the ladies in the neighborhood. This is one of the things God has given her, and her job is to do it well, under the power and wisdom of Christ

Danger of Overstepping

The Scriptures are quite plain that it is dangerous to overstep the bounds of the call of God. Uzziah reached out his hand to steady the ark of God and experienced the displeasure of the Lord (1 Chron. 13:9-10).

King Uzziah prospered mightily under the blessing of God. "But after Uzziah became powerful, his pride led to his downfall. He was unfaithful to the LORD his God, and entered the temple of the LORD to burn incense on the altar of incense" (2 Chron. 26:16). The Lord in His mercy tried to restrain Uzziah, but to no avail.

> Azariah the priest with eighty other courageous priests of the Lord followed him in. They confronted him and said, "It is not right for you, Uzziah, to burn incense to the Lord. That is for the priests, the descendants of Aaron, who have been conse-crated to burn incense. Leave the sanctuary, for you have been unfaithful; and you will not be honored by the Lord God."
> Uzziah, who had a censer in his hand ready to burn incense, became angry. While he was raging at the priests in their presence before the incense altar in the Lord'S temple, leprosy broke out on his forehead. When Azariah the chief priest and all the other priests looked at him, they saw that he had leprosy on his forehead, so they hurried him out. Indeed, he himself was eager to leave, because the Lord had afflicted him.
> King Uzziah had leprosy until the day he died. He lived in a separate house—leprous, and excluded from the temple the LORD. Jotham his son had charge of the palace and governed the people of the land (2 Chron. 26:17-21).

Saul is another classic example of a leader who overstepped the bounds of his responsibilities, to offer a burnt offering to the Lord.

When Samuel asked him about it, Saul gave an interesting answer. He implied that he really didn't want to, but in light of the circumstances, he said, "I felt compelled" (1 Sam. 13:12). Samuel's answer is straight to the point.

> "You acted foolishly," Samuel said. "You have not kept the command the LORD your God gave you; if you had, he would have established your kingdom over Israel for all time. But now your kingdom will not endure; the LORD has sought out a man after his own heart and appointed him leader of His people, because you have not kept the LORD's command" (1 Sam. 13:13-14).

The Apostle Paul said, "I consider my life worth nothing to me, if only I may finish the race and complete the task the Lord Jesus has given me—the task of testifying to the gospel of God's grace (Acts 20:24).

Leaders must not let anything—pride, envy, guilt, or any other temptation—lure them from the path of service to which God has appointed them. It is not their business to be judges or critics of what God leads others to do. Nor is it prudent for them to try to busy themselves in another person's ministry. There are plenty of snares to avoid on their own paths. There are ample roadblocks to overcome on their own paths. Let them press toward the mark that God has set for them.

Athletes know not only where the goal is, but also where the out-of-bounds markers are located. Leaders will do well to keep both in mind. Paul certainly did. He wrote: "We, however, will not boast beyond proper limits, but will confine our boasting to the field God has assigned to us, a field that reaches even to you" (2 Cor. 10:13).

Leaders Never Know It All

Leaders who know their jobs know something else as well. They know they never will get to the point where they can say they have arrived or know it all. Good leaders will continue to learn. "Wise men store up knowledge, but the mouth of a fool invites ruin" (Prov. 10:14). Note the contrast Solomon made. One kind of person continually opened his mind and laid up knowledge. The other continually opened his mouth and laid out what was on his mind.

One of the marks of good leaders is that they are teachable and eager to learn those things that will improve their performance of the task they have received from the Lord. "The discerning heart seeks knowledge, but the mouth of a fool feeds on folly" (Prov. 15:14). Effective leaders are never self-satisfied, but seek every means to become more proficient, more knowledgeable, and better able to do the job.

Solomon had the wisdom to know that being a competent leader takes more than wisdom alone. Leaders also need faith. Wisdom deals with understanding and skill. Faith goes far beyond that. It deals with what we can expect from God. To be sure, wisdom is necessary to leaders. Joseph's wise leadership and management saved an entire nation from starvation (Gen. 41:34-36). The apostles, through wise leadership and management, made provision for the needy and saved themselves from being sidetracked from their primary duties (Acts 6:1-4).

However, human understanding is not sufficient. The secret here is balance. The lazy leader might try to justify sloth by saying, "I'm just leaving the whole matter to God." The frenetic leader can work and strive to the point, practically forgetting God. Through his own wisdom, he may bring a project to a successful outcome. But it is only as wisdom is mixed with a sincere faith in God that he finds happiness and satisfaction. (See Prov. 3:5-6; 16:20.)

Since it is obvious to effective leaders that they never "arrive" in their job performance, they will continually seek ways to improve. In addition, they must develop a lifestyle of trusting God. The most important means of achieving both of these objectives is an ongoing study and application of the Word of God. "I gain understanding from your precepts; therefore I hate every wrong path" (Ps. 119:104). God's Word is the source for knowing the right thing to do and then doing it.

Seminars and books that deal with management and financial matters are helpful in building leaders' job knowledge. If they will be alert to available resources, and if they are selective, they will profit much from these materials. However, nothing beats the Word of God as a source of wisdom. "Your commands make me wiser than my enemies, for they are ever with me. I have more insight than all my teachers, for I meditate on your statutes. I have more understanding than the elders, for I obey your precepts" (Ps. 119:98-100).

Solomon called attention to another means of gaining guidance and understanding: "The way of a fool seems right to him, but a wise man listens to advice" (Prov. 12:15). Leaders should make it a practice to listen to those to whom they report, to their peers, and to those people for whom they are responsible. Time and time again, godly counsel has been used to save leaders from the serious consequences of an unwise act. Moses was certainly much better off after he heeded the counsel of Jethro (Ex. 18:14-24). Also, David was saved from his folly by the restraining counsel of Abigail (1 Sam. 25:23-32).

Some time ago, I had lunch with a missionary who is being mightily used of God among university students in Mexico. It all began at an Inter-Varsity Christian Fellowship Urbana Missionary Convention in the 1960s. While a student at the University of Texas, Dan had gone to the convention, hopeful that God would open the way for him to serve in a foreign land. He had been a Christian for something over three years, and was moderately successful in witnessing for Christ on the campus. However, he was discouraged by the lack of follow-through by those whom he had won to Christ. During the convention he met Bill, a student from Texas A & M. Bill was about his same age—and was also interested in serving the Lord as a Christian worker when he graduated. But there was one difference. This Aggie had six other students with him from A & M. He had won two of them to Christ; those had won two more, and those in turn had won two others. It was a graphic demonstration of the very thing that Dan was looking for.

Dan spent the next morning with Bill, asking him questions about his ministry at Texas A & M. He asked how he could get the kind of help in his Christian life and service that would prepare him to do the same sort of thing at the University of Texas. Bill told him that if he would drive from Bryan, Texas, to Austin once a week, he would pass along to him what he had been taught. It would be a sacrifice for the both of them. But this was exactly what Dan had longed for. So once a week for the next year, Dan drove those 80 miles to learn basic principles of witnessing and disciple making. He listened to Bill, and applied what he learned.

Today Dan is a successful missionary, surrounded by a stalwart band of Latin American laymen who are highly effective in reaching their peers for Christ and training them in a life of discipleship. Dan knows his job, and those who work with him are a highly motivated band of men and women whose morale remains high. It is a living example of Solomon's words, "He who ignores discipline comes to poverty and shame, but whoever heeds correction is honored" (Prov. 13:18)

Leaders Know Their Job

Nothing is more important for leaders than knowing their job. A few summers ago, while traveling in Europe, I had lunch in a restaurant in Oldenburg, Germany. There was a notice in the window saying that they honored the American Express card. However, when I tried to use mine to pay the bill, no one in the restaurant knew how to run the machine to record the charge.

That same summer I was driving down a motorway in Holland. A friend who was traveling with me pointed out a large, modern office building that was empty. It had been erected too close to some large gasoline storage tanks. There was an ordinance that office buildings had to be so many meters from tanks such as those. Thousands of dollars were lost. The man who issued the permit did not know his job.

Recently, our family attended a concert held in our church. The pianist had a girl sitting beside her on the piano bench to turn the pages of music. As I watched her turn the pages, I asked myself a question: *How much does a person need to know to turn the pages of a book?* Very little, of course. In fact, my little granddaughter can do that. But she couldn't have done it for the pianist at the concert. The girl at the concert had to know how to read music. There was more to it than the ability to turn pages. She had to know when to turn them. And that took training.

Leaders Finish a Job

Beginning a job can be exciting. Doing a job can be fun and fulfilling—but only if you know that there is every likelihood that you will be able to see it through to completion. To begin a job that you know is doomed to failure is demoralizing. It is the leader's responsibility to help the people accomplish the task. This presupposes he knows what he is doing and is capable of helping those who are involved with him to learn the task and bring it to a successful conclusion.

Jesus Christ is our prime example here. In His high priestly prayer He said, "I have brought you glory on earth by completing the work you gave me to do" (John 17:4). He knew his task, he completed his task, and he trained his disciples to carry on the task after his departure.

Good intentions can't replace good performance. Leaders must be competent in the job God has given them to do. In approaching their tasks, they will do well to follow Solomon's example:

> At Gibeon the Lord appeared to Solomon during the night in a dream, and God said, "Ask for whatever you want me to give you."
> Solomon answered, "You have shown great kindness to your servant, my father David, because he was faithful to you and righteous and upright in heart. You have continued this great kindness to him and have given him a son to sit on his throne this very day.
> "Now, O Lord my God, you have made your servant king in place of my father David. But I am only a little child and do not know how to carry out my duties. Your servant is here among the people you have chosen, a great people, too numerous to count or number. So give your servant a discerning heart to govern your people and to distinguish between right and wrong. For who is able to govern this great people of yours?"
> The Lord was pleased that Solomon had asked for this (1 Kings 3:5-10).

If you are responsible for an enterprise and you don't know what to do, ask God for wisdom, as Solomon did, and God will give it to you. For God wants competent leaders.

CHAPTER ELEVEN

Be a Unifying Leader

I first became aware of the advantage of working together as a team while I was helping on my brother Everett's farm during my high school years in Iowa. We had two teams of horses—Molly and Bess, and Bud and Nance. Molly was a huge horse. Bess was much smaller and much older than Molly. When we hitched them to the cultivator and headed for the field, they functioned perfectly. Molly seemed to realize that Bess needed a little extra help at times and managed somehow to give it. She would put out a bit more on the turns and sort of carry Molly along. They were easy to manage because they worked so well together.

Bud and Nance were different. They were individuals to the core, and didn't pull well together. They seemed bent on making life miserable for each other. In spite of the fact that they were younger, stronger, and filled with a greater vitality than Molly and Bess, they did not do nearly as much work in a day. Their problem was that they had never learned to function well as a team.

As I spent those summers cultivating corn, it became clear to me why our high school basketball team never did very well. Individually, we were all pretty good players. We had a good, tall center, some quick forwards, and two fairly tough guards. But we never went anywhere. We would win some games, but we were usually eliminated during the first or second game at the county tournament. Our problem? We all tried to be superstars. Being high-point man in the game seemed more important to us than winning the game. So we took spectacular shots, made fancy passes, and spent the games showing off our individual skills. The coach would try to settle us down, but we still played for personal recognition rather than team accomplishment. We loved to win, but we were our own worst enemies. We beat ourselves by our individual antics and refusal to be a functioning team. Also, I know now that our coach was letting us lead the team, instead of his being our leader.

After graduation from high school, I had the opportunity to join the Marine Corps and considered this a golden opportunity. All during my high school years, I was the skinniest guy in school and an easy mark for the school bullies. I couldn't defend myself, so I learned to outrun the guys who wanted to pick a fight. But all the while I dreamed of being big and muscular. I knew the marines were supposed to be a tough outfit, and when I was accepted, I was elated. I just knew they would make a tough guy out of me. I even had a nickname picked out for myself—Nails. Nails Eims. It had sort of a ring to it. I could just see people looking at me as I swaggered down Main Street of Neola, Iowa, and whispering to each other, "Here comes Nails!" So I joined the marines, fully expecting them to transform me into an American Tarzan.

However, quite the opposite happened. I soon discovered that they were totally consumed with the idea of ending World War II. My grand and glorious plans for myself were not even in their thinking, because they were out to defeat the enemy. So I wound up as a machine gunner on an armored amphibious tank crew.

Each of us on the crew knew his job. Mine was operating the radio and the air-cooled, 30-caliber machine gun. The driver knew his job as did the ammo man, the turret gunner, and the tank commander. No one played for himself. We were a team. Our lives depended on each other, and each of us had to do his job. By the way, I didn't become a muscular giant, and nobody ever called me Nails. My nickname in the marines was Chick. I was still the smallest one of the bunch, but as a member of that tank team, it didn't matter. I was just as important as the next guy. For we needed and trusted each other.

Solomon stated this principle succinctly and clearly: "Two are better than one, because they have a good return for their work: If one falls down, his friend can help him up. But pity the man who falls and has no one to help him up!" (Ecc. 4:9-10). If leaders can help those who colabor with them to learn this truth, they are doing a service both to the group and to the kingdom of God. A bunch of individuals going off in their own directions, doing their own things, will accomplish little. But people banded together toward a common objective, supporting each other, caring for one another, praying for and loving each other, can be a mighty force for God. Individuals who stand alone are exposed to temptations that they would not be exposed to in the midst of a team. There is mutual warmth in the fellowship, and a greater strength for spiritual warfare and for the work of Christ.

David said, "How good and pleasant it is when brothers live together in unity! . . . For there the LORD bestows His blessing, even life forevermore" (Ps. 133:1-3).

This is something I have observed over the years. People who are united in heart and mind receive the blessing of God on their lives and ministry. This united spirit is certainly one of the keys that unlocks the blessing of God and unleashes the power of God. Without this, the group invariably falls into disarray; morale sinks, and whatever motivation they had disappears.

I'm certain that unity was one of the prime reasons for the prayer of the Apostle Paul: "May the God who gives endurance and encouragement give you a spirit of unity among yourselves as you follow Christ Jesus, so that with one heart and mouth you may glorify the God and Father of our Lord Jesus Christ" (Rom. 15:5-6). Paul here revealed the grand purpose of unity: the glory of God. Obviously, the Lord is not glorified by group squabbles, disharmony, or contention. What glorifies God is like-mindedness and unity. Christian unity demonstrates that the group is controlled by the love and peace of Christ. Paul reminded the Philippians:

> Whatever happens, conduct yourselves in a manner worthy of the Gospel of Christ. Then, whether I come and see you or only hear about you in my absence, I will know that you stand firm in one spirit, contending as one man for the faith of the Gospel (Phil. 1:27).

Solomon suggested many things that influence togetherness and oneness in the group. Let's consider four destroyers and three builders of unity.

Four Destroyers of Unity

1. *Slander.* Solomon said, "He who conceals his hatred has lying

lips, and whoever spreads slander is a fool" (Prov. 10:18). One of the most effective ways to destroy another person's effectiveness for Christ is to say things that will keep people from placing their confidence in that person. This can be done through ridicule or through presenting the person in an unfavorable light by stating a suspicion as fact.

Some friends of mine were planning to go to the mission field after college. One evening this couple had a little disagreement while they were entertaining the pastor and his wife for dinner. Some months later the pastor mentioned the incident to a friend of his who happened to be on the missionary selection board. Three years later the couple applied to the board to serve overseas. As the board was discussing the possibility of the couple going overseas, the board member said, "I hear they don't get along very well together." Fortunately, the Lord had another person on the board who knew the couple and was able to state emphatically that this was not true. They got along great. Because of the slander of a man who didn't know them well, this couple was almost prohibited from going to the mission field.

2. *Anger.* Solomon said, "An angry man stirs up dissension, and a hot-tempered one commits many sins" (Prov. 29:22). "Do not make friends with a hot-tempered man, do not associate with one easily angered, or you may learn his ways and get yourself ensnared" (Prov. 22:24-25)

Anger is a contagious emotion, and can prove to be devastating to a group.

3. *Pride.* Solomon said, "Pride only breeds quarrels, but wisdom is found in those who take advice" (Prov. 13:10). Pride sparks contention over who will have the preeminence. The problem with pride is its tenaciousness. Pride is a rugged enemy, and difficult to get rid of. For us to function together in a way that glorifies God and advances His kingdom, we must deal with this enemy. Solomon said, "Pride goes before destruction, a haughty spirit before a fall. Better to be lowly in spirit and among the oppressed than to share plunder with the proud" (Prov. 16:18-19).

Shortly after I became a Christian, I met a young singer who had a great voice—and knew it. His many fans predicted he would go far. He did—straight to the bottom. After a few years of basking in the praise and adulation of the crowds and failing to maintain a practice routine, he found his voice began to lose its luster. He kept trying but without success. I have no idea where he is today.

4. *Jealousy.* Solomon said, "Anger is cruel and fury overwhelming, but who can stand before jealousy?" (Prov. 27:4). Envy is a strange thing. It can be stirred up by all the right things—a holy life, a successful ministry, a good family, well-behaved kids. All of these can fan the flames of envy in the heart.

Just before the death of Christ, Pilate said to the people, "Which one do you want me to release to you: Barabbas, or Jesus who is called Christ?" (Matt. 27:17-18). Christ's perfect life prompted envy so fierce that it led to His death. In a group, a spirit of envy can lead to all manner of problems. The leader must be on the alert for these destroyers and combat them before they destroy him, the people who work with him, and their mission.

Three Builders of Unity

1. *Love.* Solomon said, "Hatred stirs up dissension, but love covers over all wrongs" (Prov. 10:12). Hatred is like rust in the fender of a car. The rust can be eating away underneath and no one realizes it until too late. One of the pastors of our church once had a fire in his home. He put it out, and went to sleep. But a spark was still smoldering between the walls. During the night it began to burn and did a great deal of damage. That's how hatred works.

In contrast, love is right up front, right out in the open. Love leads people to cover for their friends, not to expose them. Love finds a way to overlook things rather than to take offense. Love is eager to forgive and forget. Love is inventive, creative, and imaginative, and figures out ways to make the best of things. Love is the ultimate power. It never fails.

A man was complaining to a missionary about the mission's work in Africa. "How can you go to Africa and preach to them about love when there is so much injustice in your own country?" he demanded.

The mission leader's answer was classic. "We don't go in and preach to them about love. We go in and love them."

2. *Control.* Solomon said, "A gossip betrays a confidence, but a trustworthy man keeps a secret" (Prov. 11:13). One of the laws of God was, "Do not go about spreading slander among your people" (Lev. 19:16). If you know something about another person in your group that would in any way hurt him or her if it were generally known, you should keep it to yourself.

When I was a new Christian, 1 was greatly challenged by the Jepson family in Seattle. This marvelous Christian family had a rule: never to say anything about another person unless they said something good, positive, and constructive.

Let your heart be a vault in which anything that could damage another is safely locked away, never to see the light of day. "A scoundrel plots evil, and his speech is like a scorching fire. A perverse man stirs up dissension, and a gossip separates close friends" (Prov. 16:27-28).

I'm sure James had this in mind when he wrote,

> Likewise the tongue is a small part of the body, but it makes great boasts. Consider what a great forest is set on fire by a small spark. The tongue also is a fire, a world of evil among the parts of the body. It corrupts the whole person, sets the whole course of his life on fire, and is itself set on fire by hell (James 3:5-6).

Not long ago, as I was driving to work, I saw a sanitation truck, on the back of which were these words: "Satisfaction guaranteed or double your garbage back!" I laughed—and then thought of Proverbs 17:9: "He who covers over an offense promotes love, but whoever repeats the matter separates close friends."

A true friend keeps some things to himself. I don't want my garbage back. Neither do I want it spread all over the neighborhood. A disciplined tongue can go a long way to maintaining harmony in the team. We would all do well to pray David's prayer: "Set a guard over my mouth, O LORD; keep watch over the door of my lips" (Ps. 141:3).

3. *Kindness.* Solomon said, "The tongue that brings healing is a tree of life, but a deceitful tongue crushes the spirit" (Prov. 15:4). This proverb carries the thought of controlled speech a step further. Here the person's tongue is not just harmless, but filled with a wholesome, healing, positive influence. When the person speaks, his words are a balm of blessing. "Reckless words pierce like a sword, but the tongue of the wise brings healing" (Prov. 12:18). If the air is filled with discord, the wise person brings peace to the troubled waters. Where verbal thorns abound in the garden of discontent, this person creates a paradise of joy and peace. Some people who would recoil at the thought of using a dagger against their fellowmen repeatedly pierce others with their swords of unkindness, malice, and thoughtless jesting. Kindness is a mark of the learned person.

It is also the mark of the godly person. Writing prophetic words of the coming Messiah, Isaiah recorded, "The Sovereign LORD has given me an instructed tongue, to know the word that sustains the weary. He wakens me morning by morning, wakens my ear to listen like one being taught" (Isa. 50:4). Kindness should be a law that governs our speech. "She speaks with wisdom, and faithful instruction is on her tongue" (Prov. 31:26).

A Leader's Responsibilities

Solomon suggested four responsibilities for the leader, which contribute directly to maintaining the harmony and unity needed to keep people on target and motivated to accomplish the task.

1. *Integrity.* Solomon said, "The lips of the righteous nourish many, but fools die for lack of judgment" (Prov. 10:21). If leaders are diligent to nourish their people, to help them learn, to assist them in their work, and to teach them the Word, leaders will be laying the foundation of harmony and peace. The people will know they are becoming wealthy in the truest sense of the word. Paul spoke of being "poor, yet making many rich" (2 Cor. 6:10). The people will be nourished in the words of faith as their leader draws from the treasure of the Word that dwells richly in his or her heart (Col. 3:16). The leader and the people will experience the true leadership described by Malachi:

True instruction was in his mouth and nothing false was found on his lips. He walked with me in peace and uprightness, and turned many from sin. For the lips of a priest ought to preserve knowledge, and from his mouth men should seek instruction—because he is the messenger of the LORD Almighty (Mal. 2:6-7).

2. *Restraint.* Solomon said, "A gentle answer turns away wrath, but a harsh word stirs up anger" (Prov. 15:1). Leaders must keep their cool in the midst of tumult and dissension. If they respond in kind to heated words, they will do nothing but spread the flame of dissent and disunity. If they yield to the temptation to justify themselves, put other people in their place, or insist on the last word, they have lost the battle for peace.

Restraint is a peacemaker. Those who exercise it win two battles— over themselves and over others. A peacemaker applies Romans 12:19: "Do not take revenge, my friends, but leave room for God's wrath, for it is written: 'It is mine to avenge; I will repay,' says the Lord."

The leader's tongue must be disciplined and dedicated to God. "A man's wisdom gives him patience; it is to his glory to overlook an offense" (Prov. 19:11).

3. *Good humor.* Solomon said, "A cheerful heart is good medicine, but a crushed spirit dries up the bones" (Prov. 17:22). The thoughts expressed in Hebrews 1:9 have always been a source of wonder to me. "You have loved righteousness and hated wickedness; therefore God, your God, has set you above your companions by anointing you with the oil of joy." Even though Jesus was a Man of sorrows and acquainted with grief, He also exhibited more gladness than anyone around Him did.

Recently, I attended a rather large convention of Christian leaders. I recall seeking out one man who was full of the blessing of God. I knew he would be—it is his lifestyle. He rejoices even in tribulation. God has used his merry heart to inspire and motivate me. I also recall studiously avoiding another man who was there. He is known for his gloom and doom. In every contact I have had with him, he has exuded a cranky, complaining spirit. The contrast was vivid.

4. *Friendship*. Solomon said, "A friend loves at all times, and a brother is born for adversity" and "There is a friend who sticks closer than a brother" (Prov. 17:17; 18:24). A good leader is friendly to those in the group. I have read management books and military manuals than warn against this: "Don't get too close to your people." Of course this is nonsense. Jesus said, "I no longer call you servants, because a servant does not know his master's business. Instead, I have called you friends, for everything that I learned from my Father I have made known to you" (John 15:15). How close is He to us? Closer than a brother! He indwells us!

Leaders who hold themselves aloof will stimulate a chill in the group. Leaders who reach out in friendship will generate warmth. It is certainly worth the effort for leaders to love the unlovely, befriend the unfriendly, cheer those who are down, and compliment those who are giving their all. In so doing, they will build a team whose morale and motivation will be used of the Spirit of God to enlarge the kingdom of God.

Mutual Need

The value of a united team cannot be overstated. Together, all of us are better than some of us. All of us will do more and do it better than a few isolated individuals. I have a friend who teaches in a unique graduate school. The purpose of the school is to demonstrate to the pupils the value of a team effort. A myriad of problems is presented for the class to solve. In one case, each class member is given the problem to work on individually. After a specified time, each person is placed on a team to talk the problem over—share ideas and then work on the problem together. Without exception, when the team tackles the problem together, the members arrive at better solutions than any of the individuals did when they worked on it separately.

God has placed us in a body—the body of Christ. It is His purpose to demonstrate to us our interdependence on each other:

> As it is, there are many parts, but one body. The eye cannot say to the hand, "I don't need you!" And the head cannot say to the feet, "I don't need you!" . . . But God has combined the

members of the body and has given greater honor to the parts that lacked it, so that there should be no division in the body, but that its parts should have equal concern for each other. If one part suffers, every part suffers with it; if one part is honored, every part rejoices with it (1 Cor. 12:20-21, 24-26).

CHAPTER TWELVE

Be a Working Leader

Solomon was a multitalented individual. He was a builder, a leader, a manager, a decision maker, a goal setter, and much more. He was wise. He modeled the attributes of one who could maintain morale and motivate the masses. He built a huge fortune and ruled a mighty kingdom.

> Not only was the Teacher wise, but also he imparted knowledge to the people. He pondered and searched out and set in order many proverbs. The Teacher searched to find just the right words, and what he wrote was upright and true.
> The words of the wise are like goads, their collected sayings like firmly embedded nails—given by one Shepherd (Ecc. 12:9-11).

As we reflect on Solomon's life, however, we are struck with an awesome truth. All that he had has since vanished. His mighty fleet, his great herds, his glorious temple, his great wealth, his beautiful home, and his kingdom are gone. But that which he taught remains.

If leaders are wise, they will glean a great lesson from this. There is much they can do—most of which will decay and vanish with the coming of tomorrow. But that which they teach and build into the lives of people will last, especially if their vision is strong enough to project itself beyond the immediate. And, if leaders understand the necessity of teaching those they instruct to be teachers of others, others in turn will continue to repeat the process.

This was the genius of the Apostle Paul. He summarizes his vision: "And the things you have heard me say in the presence of many witnesses entrust to reliable men who will also be qualified to teach others" (2 Tim. 2:2). In this passage, Paul set forth his aim. He was committed to equipping laborers who could carry on the ministry that God had entrusted to him—the ministry of evangelizing the lost, establishing the saved, equipping spiritually qualified laborers for the harvest, and training competent leaders to carry on the ministry when he eventually would pass from the scene.

In the chapters of this book, we have discussed many things that a Christian leader should do. But what is the objective of all these things? These attributes and objectives of an effective leader are not ends in themselves. They are tools for accomplishing the task. This chapter presents the goal of Christian leadership—multiplying laborers for the vast and overripe harvest.

Unless people are won to Christ, there is no one to establish in the faith. But if a leader aims his personal ministry primarily at evangelizing the lost, he will accomplish only what one person can do. If he aims his ministry at multiplying laborers, he will see what a host of competent, trained, motivated men and women can accomplish.

The Leader as Laborer

Does that mean leaders should not evangelize the lost or establish the saved? Of course not. They themselves are laborers in the harvest and must never forget that. If they quit laboring in the harvest, they will lose their prime teaching tool—setting an example for others to follow. Let us be very clear on this point—leaders are laborers all the days of their lives.

When the Bible refers to a laborer, what is it describing? For a partial answer to that question, we can look at a statement of Jesus.

When He saw the crowds, He had compassion on them, because they were harassed and helpless, like sheep without a shepherd. Then he said to his disciples, "The harvest is plentiful but the workers are few. Ask the Lord of the harvest, therefore, to send out workers into his harvest field" (Matt. 9:36-38).

A laborer is one who is directly related to the harvest. We recognize there are laborers of many kinds in the work of the church, but for our purposes we will concentrate our attention on this one kind—the harvest worker.

The word that Jesus used is the word *ergatees*, which means "a farmer, one who works in the field." This truth is hard for some Christian leaders to accept. They visualize themselves at the other end of the spectrum. Rather than being out in the hot, dusty field doing the work of field hands, they see themselves behind huge desks in air-conditioned offices, jotting off memos to others that labor. But the Bible makes no provision for this kind of leader. The Seventy were laborers. The apostles were laborers. Jesus Himself was a laborer. "As long as it is day, we must do the work of him who sent me. Night is coming, when no one can work" (John 9:4). Paul told Timothy, "Do your best to present yourself to God as one approved, a workman who does not need to be ashamed and who correctly handles the word of truth" (2 Tim. 2:15).

Jesus led his team into a vast, overripe harvest. "After Jesus had finished instructing his twelve disciples, he went on from there to teach and preach in the towns of Galilee (Matt. 11:1).

Paul did the same. "As his custom was, Paul went into the synagogue, and on three Sabbath days he reasoned with them from the Scriptures" (Acts 17:2).

Leaders who would follow the example of Christ and of the disciples whom He selected and trained must labor and train others to do the same. Paul says we are laborers together with God (1 Cor. 3:9). He wrote to the Thessalonians about their work of faith and labor of love (1 Thes. 1:3). He called Epaphroditus his brother and fellow-worker (Phil. 2:25). He admonished the church: "Now we ask you, brothers, to respect those who work hard among you, who are over you in the Lord and who admonish you" (1 Thes. 5:12). He called elders "those whose work is preaching and teaching" (1 Tim. 5:17). He reminded the Colossians of Epaphras who was "always wrestling in prayer for you" (Col. 4:12). We are called to be laborers.

We gather from all this that witnessing is work, discipling is work, training laborers is work, leadership is work, preaching is work, and praying is work. All of these are directly related to the plentiful harvest.

The Leader as Equipper

Leaders are laborers, first, last, and always. But more than that, they are laborers plus. For they are laborers who also train others to labor. Not only are they skilled in winning the lost and building up the saved, but they also know how to equip others to do the same. So we might call them equippers.

An equipper is one who can help disciples become laborers. The Apostle Paul wrote that God "gave some to be apostles, some to be prophets, some to be evangelists, and some to be pastors and teachers, to prepare God's people for works of service, so that the body of Christ may be built up" (Eph. 4:11-12).

A study of the Greek word *katartizo*, here translated "prepare," opens up a treasure chest of practical help for the leader who is serious about becoming a wise master builder, a skilled equipper, a faithful man or woman who is able to teach others. Its shades of meaning are many. Greek scholars tell us that *katartizo* means "to complete thoroughly, repair, adjust, fit, frame, mend, make perfect, perfectly join together, prepare, restore, and furnish completely."

Paul reminded the Ephesians that God had provided them with certain divinely appointed leadership whose job it was to get them ready to do high-quality work in the kingdom of God.

It is the leader's task to ensure that the workers are skillful in their use of the Bible, highly motivated, and committed to the task of laboring long and hard in the vast, overripe harvest that surrounds them.

The same word is used in 1 Peter 5:10: "And the God of all grace, who called you to his eternal glory in Christ, after you have suffered a little while, will himself restore you and make you strong, firm and steadfast." Translated here as "restore," it means "to fit you out completely," "to make you whole," "to make you what you ought to be."

Don Enright is a friend of mine who lives in Colorado Springs. He is an outstanding artist who specializes in drawing wild animals. For years he has concentrated his talent on the bighorn sheep that inhabit the Rocky Mountains. A few years ago, he decided to broaden his range and include the wild beasts of Africa. To prepare for the task, he took his camera and joined an African safari. At base camp they equipped or outfitted their party for their trek into the bush. They needed medicines, first-aid equipment, food, tents, rifles, ammunition, and men to carry the supplies. That's how Peter used the word *katartizo*. As one would outfit a safari, the God of all grace—the Author and Finisher of our faith—works to outfit our lives for His glory.

The word is used again in Mark 1:19 and is translated "preparing." Here the word means "to repair, overhaul, to make ready for use." James and John were repairing their nets and getting them in order.

In this sense, the leader is likened to a repairman. When we need car repair, in some cases we need just a minor adjustment— replacing a fuse or tightening a bolt. But sometimes it means a major overhaul. The mechanic must be able to do both in order to enable the automobile to function at its best. And so the leader must have the compassion and skill to take the broken or bruised lives and make whatever major or minor repairs are needed to get them functioning again in perfect order.

Paul expressed a similar idea to the Thessalonians: "Night and day we pray most earnestly that we may see you again and supply what is lacking in your faith" (1 Thes. 3:10).

When my youngest son was in junior high school, he was given a large poster and a box of colored pencils. He was supposed to follow the instructions and paint the picture. There were scores of colors involved and it was quite a complicated task. So he began. Night after night he worked on his project. He would do the reds, then the blues, then the greens, and so on. One by one he filled in the gaps and finally the picture was complete. It took weeks to complete, but he finally made it, and it was beautiful. That's the thrust of the word here. Possibly, there are certain misunderstood doctrines that the leader must teach simply and clearly. He may strengthen people's faith in the promises of God or help them learn how to study the Bible for themselves. Wherever there are gaps, the leader must take whatever action is necessary to see that they are filled in.

In Hebrews 11:3, we see another meaning of *katartizo*: "By faith we understand that the universe was formed at God's command, so that what is seen was not made out of what was visible." Formed means "to arrange, to place in proper order." In the beginning, the world was without form and void. There was confusion and emptiness. But out of this shapeless, useless mass, this rough draft, God brought forth a world of perfect order that functions perfectly according to His divine plan and law. This should be of great encouragement to the leader. If God can do it with His world, He can do it with His people. I have talked with leaders who looked on their people and saw confused, useless, empty lives. God's power, His wisdom, His Word, and His Spirit can work mighty and dramatic changes. Confusion can be turned to purpose. Uselessness can be changed to productivity.

Luke gives us another facet of the word. "A student is not above his teacher, but everyone who is fully trained will be like his teacher" (Luke 6:40). Here is the idea of growth. Leaders are to help the people grow in grace and the likeness of Christ. They must teach them to pray and to read and memorize the Word, in order to establish a daily and meaningful fellowship with the Savior. All too often leaders rely only on their teaching to accomplish the task. And all too often, that doesn't work.

Yes, people need to be taught. But Jude added the missing ingredient. "But you, dear friends, build yourselves up in your most holy faith and pray in the Holy Spirit. Keep yourselves in God's love as you wait for the mercy of our Lord Jesus Christ to bring you to eternal life" (Jude 20-21).

People must be taught means to mature and to keep themselves in the love of God. If leaders can help their people learn how to dig into the Word for themselves, to write it on the tables of their hearts through Scripture memory, to establish the practice of morning prayer and Bible reading, they will do much to help their people grow and develop into all that God wants them to be.

In Galatians 6:1, we see another use of *katartizo*. "Brothers, if someone is caught in a sin, you who are spiritual should restore him gently. But watch yourself, or you also may be tempted." Here the leader who is controlled by the Holy Spirit must redirect the wanderer and gently set him right. The word is used here in a medical sense, to reset, as in the case of a dislocated bone. A dislocated limb cannot function properly. A person out of joint in the body of Christ could be lost to effective service in the kingdom of God.

Some years ago the following notice appeared in our newspaper:

THREE YOUTHS HURT IN AUTO ACCIDENT

Three youths were injured when their car left U.S. 24 near Green Mountain Falls and plummeted 323 feet down an embankment, rolling over twice, according to the State Patrol. Randy S. Eims, 17, was admitted to Penrose Hospital with a broken foot. Eims is in satisfactory condition, a hospital spokesman said.

While Randy was sleeping in the back seat, the Volkswagen convertible in which he was a passenger suddenly left the road and rolled end over end down the embankment. I arrived at the hospital in time to see the doctor make arrangements to pop the bone back into place. He had the knowledge and the skill and the gentleness to do the job right. The next few weeks were quite an education for Virginia and me. Here was a muscular young man, a terror on the soccer field, a tiger on the tennis courts, and a picture of graceful coordination on the ski slopes, practically helpless. But eventually the foot healed and he was back in action.

That's the idea in this passage. The Apostle Paul was not speaking of a person in hot pursuit of sin, but of one who was injured. Now this person was crippled and needed to be restored to health and service by someone who would manifest the fruit of the Spirit—love, gentleness, and meekness being prime requisites.

In Hebrews 13:20-21 we see *katartizo* relating to the will of God.

May the God of peace, who through the blood of the eternal covenant brought back from the dead our Lord Jesus, that great Shepherd of the sheep, equip you with everything good for doing his will, and may he work in us what is pleasing to him, through Jesus Christ to whom be glory for ever and ever. Amen.

It is true that people will not grow to their fullest maturity, or come to their place of greatest service for Christ, if they are constantly in doubt as to the will of God for their lives. But if they are confident that they know what God wants them to do, they are highly motivated to receive the instruction and training they need. Leaders who are ready, willing, and able to help prepare others to do the will of God will render a great service to His kingdom. Some people need to discover God's will. Others need to prepare themselves to do it. With yet others, it is a combination of both. Once again we clearly see the need for discernment, patience, and skill in the life of leaders. They must spend much time on their knees before God, and with the open Bible, if they would be effective in this ministry of equipping others to discern and accomplish God's will for their lives.

Paul used the word again in his letter to the Corinthians: "I appeal to you, brothers, in the name of our Lord Jesus Christ, that all of you agree with one another so that there may be no divisions among you and that you may be perfectly united in mind and thought" (1 Cor. 1:10). This speaks of the unity of believers. A bickering, jealous, suspicious body of believers is of little use to the Holy Spirit in advancing the cause of Christ. Jesus prayed, "That all of them may be one, Father, just as you are in me and I am in you. May they also be in us so that the world may believe that you have sent me" (John 17:21). The prayer of Paul was that there would be no factions and divisions, but that believers would be solidly joined together in mind and thought. To build unity is not easy. To keep it can be even harder. The Devil is always on the lookout to drive some wedge between the brothers and sisters in Christ and render them useless to the purpose of God. To keep the unity of the Spirit in the bond of peace requires work, prayer, admonition, and encouragement.

The last verse we will consider is 2 Corinthians 13:9. "We are glad whenever we are weak but you are strong; and our prayer is for your perfection." The thought here is the all-around strengthening and development of Christian character.

Perseverance

Katartizo has to do with "fitting out," "overhauling," "filling in the gaps," "placing in order," and in a medical sense, "setting a joint in place." All of this is done for the purpose of helping people do the work that God has given them, to help them grow strong in the Lord and the power of His might, to discern and do the will of God, to live in unity, and to develop godly Christian character.

There are two ways leaders can look at these tasks—in despair or in dependence. They can see the job, and throw up their hands in frustration. Or they can see their limitations, their lack of experience and knowledge, and ask, "Who is sufficient for these things?"

The Apostle Paul said: "Not that we are competent in ourselves to claim anything for ourselves, but our competence comes from God. He has made us competent as ministers of a new covenant—not of the letter but of the Spirit; for the letter kills, but the Spirit gives life" (2 Cor. 3:5-6). Leaders must persevere and remain at the task they have been given.

One of the finest examples I ever saw of perseverance was on the island of Fiji. My wife and I were in a bus on our way to the airport. We had gotten a late start and the driver was doing all he could to make up time and get the passengers to their flight. The rain was blowing in through the broken windows as we bounced along. At the foot of the hill, we came behind a slow-moving cement truck. Our driver was clearly agitated at this stroke of bad fortune and tried to pass. But to no avail. Oncoming traffic kept him behind the cement truck for miles and miles. Finally, with a break in the traffic, the driver passed the truck, and we bounced down the road at top speed. But then the driver spotted a small boy standing in the middle of the road and carrying a tin sign. He was on school patrol, to stop the traffic and permit the children to cross the road. The little tin sign said, "Stop." But our bus driver was in no mood to stop.

The lad saw him coming at breakneck speed and started to run for the ditch. But the boy's sense of duty prevailed. He turned, faced the oncoming bus, and stood his ground. At the last minute when he saw he could not win, the driver slammed on his brakes.

The bus slid to a stop and the uniformed school children passed safely across the road. The lad had persevered and won the test of wills. By the way, we arrived at the airport just in time to get on the plane.

Reward

Let me assure you of this: equipping people to be and do their best for Christ may be a tough, demanding, and sometimes thankless job, but it is worth it. The truth of this was driven home to me some years ago when I was speaking at a servicemen's conference on the island of Okinawa. The chaplain had secured an abandoned radar site for our meetings. No other religious group had ever been permitted to use the site. Chaplain Boggs had put in many hours over many months and logged over 1,000 phone calls to get the place for us. On Saturday morning he came out to the conference and told us why he had worked so hard for us.

Some years before, he had been stationed at Fort Riley, Kansas. One day, two soldiers came into his office and asked if they could help him in his work. They wanted to do evangelism in the barracks and form some Bible study groups. Chaplain Boggs was delighted. In a matter of weeks there were 19 men involved, and soon he was preaching to two full services on Sunday morning, rather than to one that was half empty. The outfit then was ordered to Vietnam, and on the ship going over, the two men who had talked with the chaplain at Fort Riley came to him and asked if they could have a Bible study. Chaplain Boggs checked with the captain and secured permission.

A year later when the chaplain returned to the States, a minister came into his office and laid three letters on his desk. The letters were from the minister's son. This is what they said.

"Dear Dad, some guys on board ship have invited me to a Bible study. Think I'll go—thought it would please you."

The second said, "Dear Dad, we're in Vietnam now and I'm leading a Navigator Bible study."

The third one said, "Dear Dad, tomorrow is a big operation—don't know if I'll make it back. If I don't, thank The Navigators and Chaplain Boggs." Then the father asked if Chaplain Boggs would preach the funeral service for his son.

After telling us this story, Chaplain Boggs exhorted us to give our lives to equipping others to become laborers for Christ. He had seen how the Lord had used the two men who had first come to him at Fort Riley. God had used them to revive his chapel services, to inspire many people to study the Word on their own, and to restore the minister's son to fellowship with the Lord. At one time, somebody had made an investment in the lives of these two men that paid rich dividends. As I listened to Chaplain Boggs tell the story, I was struck with the fact that the two soldiers in Chaplain Boggs' story were not professional Christian workers, but just two ordinary guys doing what somebody had previously equipped them to do.

Let me urge you to do the same. If there is one thing this world needs, it is spiritually qualified laborers who are proficient in bringing people to Christ, and who know:

- how to help them grow in the faith through daily fellowship with Christ;
- how to teach people how to study the Bible;
- how to memorize Scripture and encourage others to do the same;
- how to pray and help others establish a vital prayer life;

and so on down the list of the spiritual basics. But there is one catch. You as leader must be setting the example.

If you give yourself to people in this way, you will be a leader who maintains motivation and morale among your people at the highest level. You will be investing your life in equipping laborers for the harvest all over the world. "The harvest is plentiful, but the workers are few" (Luke 10:2). Like every Christian you have a decision to make. You can watch others work, or you can join the ranks of God's laborers.

Personal and Group Study Guide

For Personal Study

Settle into your favorite chair with your Bible, a pen or pencil, and this book. Read a chapter, marking portions that seem significant to you. Write in the margins. Note where you agree, disagree, or question the author. Look up relevant Scripture passages. Then turn to the questions listed in this study guide. If you want to trace your progress with a written record, use a notebook to record your answers, thoughts, feelings, and further questions. Refer to the text and to the Scriptures as you allow the questions to enlarge your thinking. And pray. Ask God to give you a discerning mind for truth, an active concern for others, and a greater love for Himself.

For Group Study

Plan ahead. Before meeting with your group, read and mark the chapter as if you were preparing for personal study. Glance through the questions making mental notes of how you might contribute to your group's discussion. Bring a Bible and the text to your meeting.

Arrange an environment that promotes discussion. Comfortable chairs arranged in a casual circle invite people to talk with each other. It says, "We are here to listen and respond to each other—and to learn together." If you are the leader, simply be sure to sit where you can have eye contact with each person.

Promptness counts. Time is as valuable to many people as money. If the group runs late (because of a late start), these people will feel as robbed as if you had picked their pockets. So, unless you have mutual agreement, begin and end on time.

Involve everyone. Group learning works best if everyone participates more or less equally. If you are a natural talker, pause before you enter the conversation. Then ask a quiet person what he or she thinks. If you are a natural listener, don't hesitate to jump into the discussion. Others will benefit from your thoughts but only if you speak them. If you are the leader, be careful not to dominate the session. Of course, you will have thought about the study ahead of time, but don't assume that people are present just to hear you—as flattering as that may feel. Instead, help group members to make their own discoveries. Ask the questions, but insert your own ideas only as they are needed to fill gaps.

Pace the study. The questions for each session are designed to last about one hour. Early questions form the framework for later discussion, so don't rush by so quickly that you miss valuable foundation. Later questions, however, often speak of the here and now. So don't dawdle so long at the beginning that you leave no time to "get personal." While the leader must take responsibility for timing the flow of questions, it is the job of each person in the group to assist in keeping the study moving at an even pace.

Pray for each other—together and alone. Then watch God's hand at work in all of your lives.

Notice that each session includes the following features:

Session Topic—a brief statement summarizing the session.

Community Builder—an activity to get acquainted with the session topic and/or with each other.

Questions—a list of questions to encourage individual or group discovery and application.

Prayer Focus—suggestions for turning one's learning into prayer.

Optional Activities—supplemental ideas that will enhance the study.

Assignment—activities or preparation to complete prior to the next session.

Chapter One

Be a Responsible Leader

Session Topic

Effective leaders build motivation and morale by accepting responsibility for the group's actions.

Community Builder (Choose One)

1. Describe a time when a leader left you to take the blame for a group problem. How did you feel about the group? How did you feel about the leader?

2. Other than Jesus, who is the leader (living or dead) you admire most? Why?

Group Discovery Questions

1. Eims suggests that leaders who refuse to accept responsibility for the actions of those they lead destroy their morale. Why do you think this is so?

2. In your experience, what kind of personality traits lead people to avoid their responsibilities as leaders? What kinds of personality traits lead people to accept their responsibilities as leaders?

3. Eims says, "The heart, being sinister and deceptive, declares evil to be good and good to be evil. We all imagine our hearts to be better than they are. In fact, the human heart will allow us to vindicate ourselves in self-deception" (p. 13). How do you feel about that statement? How should leaders address the problem of their deceitful hearts?

4. What responsibility do leaders have to rebuke or correct those they lead?

5. What do you find to be the most difficult aspects of correcting people who have made mistakes?

6. How would you distinguish decisiveness on the part of a leader from impulsiveness?

7. How can you as a leader distinguish criticism that is constructive from criticism that is harmful to your group?

8. In what kinds of situations are leaders tempted to conceal or withhold the truth from those they lead?

9. How do people react to leaders who have been found to be dishonest?

10. How do you react to leaders who treat people unfairly?

11. What should you as a leader accept responsibility for in your group? Why?

12. Create a written description (about 25 words) of a responsible leader. Begin your description "A responsible leader will. . . ." If your group is large, do this in subgroups of three and then share the subgroup results.

Prayer Focus

- Confess any failures to accept full responsibility as a leader.

- Ask God to clarify in your understanding any steps you need to take to become a more responsible leader.

- Make specific commitments to God about ways in which you will fulfill your leadership responsibilities.

Optional Activities

1. Interview a leader whom you respect and admire about how he or she accepts responsibility to give correction, act decisively, listen to criticism, maintain honesty, and treat people without favoritism.

2. Ask a trusted and frank coworker or supervisor to evaluate your level of leadership responsibility in the areas of correcting, acting decisively, accepting criticism, reacting honestly, and being fair.

Assignment

1. Write an action plan to strengthen your most important weakness in accepting responsibility as a leader.

2. Read chapter 2 of *Be a Motivational Leader* and preview the Group Discovery Questions.

3. Read 2 Peter 1:3-11 in a different translation each day.

Chapter Two

Be a Growing Leader

Session Topic

Effective leaders commit themselves to the fundamental principles of personal growth.

Community Builder (Choose One)

1. Tell the group about a period in your life when you experienced remarkable spiritual growth. Why did you grow so much then?

2. In what area of your life are you experiencing the most personal growth now? Why is this happening?

Group Discovery Questions

1. What are some of the basic concepts of spiritual growth that you learned as a young Christian that you need to focus on to keep growing now?

2. Eims observes, "One of the greatest dangers of pride is that it implies overconfidence and in turn breeds a careless attitude toward spiritual realities" (p. 21). How can pride become an obstacle to your growth as a leader?

3. What does this proverb have to say about laziness: "One who is slack in his work is brother to one who destroys" (Prov. 18:9)?

4. Do you struggle with laziness, or do you tend to work too much? How should you try to correct this tendency?

5. How do you think humility before God leads to personal and spiritual growth?

6. In what areas of your life do you find it difficult to be humble? Why do you think this is so?

7. What do you think is the connection between your personal holiness and your growth as an effective leader?

8. Eims offers this definition: "Prudence is the ability to govern and discipline oneself by the use of reason" (p. 28). What are some areas of life in which you need to be prudent in order to keep growing?

9. Eims focuses on spiritual growth in this chapter. How do you think healthy spiritual growth contributes to your growth as a leader?

10. What practical steps would you take to deal with pride as a barrier to growth?

11. If a leader recognizes that a sinful habit is stunting his or her growth, how would you recommend that he or she deal with the habit and replace it with growth?

12. Eims writes (p. 19), "Leaders must continue to grow in both their personal and spiritual lives, and in their ability to perform their jobs." How can you stimulate growth in your friendships? Your spiritual disciplines? Your ability to perform your job?

Prayer Focus

- Read Paul's prayer for growth in Colossians 1:9-14.

- Pray that you would "crave pure spiritual milk, so that by it you may grow up in your salvation" (1 Peter 2:2).

- Ask God for companions on your journey of growth to stimulate you and hold you accountable.

Assignment

1. Write a growth objective for each of these areas of your life: spiritual maturity, mental development, physical wellbeing, and career advancement.

2. Read chapter 3 of Be a Motivational Leader and preview the Group Discovery Questions.

3. Meditate on Philippians 2, which is packed with exemplary leaders. Notice how Timothy and Epaphroditus followed the example of Jesus by following the example of Paul.

Chapter Three

Be an Exemplary Leader

Session Topic

Effective leaders serve as ongoing examples to those they lead in order to motivate and train them.

Community Builder (Choose One)

1. Recall a complicated process (such as a sport or craft) that you learned from the example of others rather than from reading or listening to instructions. Describe how it happened.

2. Which of your parents (or other family member) taught you by doing things with you? What do you still do like that person?

Group Discovery Questions

1. Eims says a leader should be exemplary. Do you think he means just that the leader should be an example or that the leader

should be outstanding? Why do you think so?

2. Eims suggests that too much Christian instruction is telling aimed at mature disciples rather than showing aimed at young Christians. How do you react to that?

3. What aspects of Christian living and doctrine do you think need to be taught more by example than by word? Why did you select these?

4. Why is it easier to tell people about the Christian life than it is to show them how to live it?

5. What aspects of your Christian life did you learn by observing the example of someone else?

6. What aspects of your job did you learn by watching the example of someone else?

7. What things need to be true of a leader's Christian life and commitment before he or she should try to lead by example?

8. Which of your Christian disciplines would you like to improve in order to become a better example as a leader?

9. How will a joyous, positive attitude increase the effectiveness of your example as a leader? How will a complaining, negative attitude limit your effectiveness as an example?

10. In the leadership position you occupy, what are you teaching by example to those who follow you?

11. What areas of your life and commitment would you need to work on to become a more effective leader by example?

12. Who are people in your life who have been influenced for good or bad by the example of your life and leadership? How do you feel about the influence of your example?

Prayer Focus

- Read Philippians 2:5-11 about the power of Jesus' example to shape our lives. Tell God some of the things you have learned from the example of Jesus.

- Pray for the courage, commitment, and discipline you need to accept the challenge of leading by the example of your Christian life.

- Ask God to bless your church with leaders who can disciple you by their example.

Assignment

1. Guide one of your friends (or children) through a process you know well using Dawson Trotman's five-step program: (1) Tell him what, (2) Tell him why, (3) Show him how, (4) Help him get started, and (5) Help him keep going (p. 32). What did you learn about being an example?

2. Read chapter 4 of *Be a Motivational Leader* and preview the Group Discovery Questions.

3. Read Hebrews 12:1-4 and jot down ways you have been inspired to excellence by Jesus' life.

Optional Activities

1. Interview three or four people about the characteristics they want their groups' leaders to exemplify for them.

2. Write a letter of gratitude to someone whose life has been a powerful example of Christian living for you.

Four

Be an Inspiring Leader

Session Topic

Effective leaders need to display the kind of character that inspires followers to excellence.

Community Builder (Choose One)

1. Who in your life has been frank enough to point out your faults and loving enough to get away with it without offending you?

2. When you hear a well-known speaker or are in a group with an important person, do you make a point of meeting that person or are you embarrassed to approach him or her? Why do you think you approach authorities the way you do?

Group Discovery Questions

1. Read Proverbs 27:5-6. How can loving frankness on the part of leaders inspire high morale in an organization?

2. How does loving frankness differ from unkindness and hostility?

3. When have you seen loving frankness inspire a person to greater excellence?

4. Read Proverbs 17:17. We all know that followers should be loyal to leaders. What are some important ways leaders can express their loyalty to those who follow them?

5. When have you seen a leader show unusual loyalty to those he or she leads?

6. What do you think are the best ways to use praise to inspire people?

7. How do you respond to praise? How does praise affect your vanity and your ability to give credit to God for your successes?

8. "Some people have the capacity to be trained as leaders, and others don't," Eims asserts (p. 46). In your opinion, what kind of people respond to inspiring leadership and in turn become leaders?

9. Read Proverbs 27:17. What disciplines do you think you need to practice to become a leader sharp enough to sharpen others? In what ways do you think God will use your personality and gifts to sharpen others?

10. As you reflect on leaders who have inspired you to excellence, what was it about them that you found inspiring? On the other hand, what kinds of leaders have destroyed your motivation toward excellence?

11. What are some changes you could make in your leadership style that would make you a more inspiring leader?

Prayer Focus

• Read Paul's inspiring prayer in Philippians 1:3-11.

• Pray for people under your leadership who need to be inspired to greater commitment and excellence.

• Ask God for the commitment and the discipline necessary to be a more inspirational leader.

Optional Activities

1. Eims identifies four stages in the development of Christian disciples: new Christian, growing disciple, budding laborer, and prospective leader. Each needs a different kind of inspiration. Categorize the people in your group into levels of development and assess the kind of inspiration each subgroup needs.

2. Write a profile of the leadership trainee your group or church needs to be working with.

Assignment

1. Identify a person in your group who needs inspiration, and plan a contact in which you can express at least one inspiring leadership quality.

2. Read chapter 5 of *Be a Motivational Leader* and preview the Group Discovery Questions.

3. Examine Exodus 18:13-27 for the aspects of efficiency discussed in *Be a Motivational Leader.*

Five

Be an Efficient Leader

Session Topic

Effective leaders manage all of their resources to achieve maximum results from everyone's efforts.

Community Builder (Choose One)

1. When were you punished as a child for doing something that no one had ever told you was wrong? How did you feel about the situation and the one who punished you?

2. Who is the most efficient person you know? Give an example of that person's efficiency.

Group Discovery Questions

1. What are some things leaders can do to clarify their sense of direction from God?

2. How has God given you direction in your leadership responsibilities?

3. What sorts of things do leaders need to communicate regularly and clearly to those they lead?

4. Whom have you known who was particularly skillful in communicating as a leader? Explain your choice(s).

5. What personal qualities does a leader need to be an effective delegator?

6. To what kind of person can a leader successfully delegate responsibility?

7. What do you find most difficult about delegating authority? How do you deal with this difficulty?

8. What kind of help should leaders be available to provide for those to whom they have given jobs?

9. How can you as a leader make time in your schedule to help someone to whom you have given a responsibility?

10. How do you think a leader should evaluate the performance of his or her workers?

11. What are the best and the worst job evaluation situations you have been involved in? What made them rank high and low?

12. What do you think frustrated, overwhelmed leaders should do to restore their efficiency?

13. Not everyone is naturally organized and efficient. How do you think leaders who aren't gifted in administration can increase efficiency in their organizations?

14. What aspects of efficient leadership would you like to see strengthened in your life? Why?

Prayer Focus

* Read Paul's prayer and report concerning the Thessalonian church in 1 Thessalonians 1:2-10. Notice the elements of efficient leadership illustrated in this passage.

* Pray for the efficiency of your leadership and of those whom you lead.

* Pray for the leaders of your church that they will be able to minister efficiently.

Optional Activity

* Divide a sheet of paper into two columns. In one column list your strengths as an efficient leader, and in the other column your weaknesses. At the bottom of the page (or on another sheet), write three suggestions for improving your efficiency as a leader.

Assignment

1. Clarify your understanding of the direction of God for your life

by writing it out. Identify the general area in which God has prepared you to serve and add any particulars about that service of which you are confident.

2. Read chapter 6 of *Be a Motivational Leader* and preview the Group Discovery Questions.

3. Read 1 Peter 5:1-4 and list as many characteristics of shepherd leadership as you can find in those verses.

Six

Be a Caring Leader

Session Topic

Effective leaders focus on opportunities to help those they lead grow and succeed.

Community Builder (Choose One)

1. Tell about a time you saw someone have difficulty managing one or more animals What should that person have done differently?

2. Who is the person who has motivated you to excel by the way he or she cared about you? How did you know this person cared for you?

Group Discovery Questions

1. How can leaders learn about the people they lead so they can care for them?

2. Read John 10:10-13. How do both the thief and the hireling reveal their self-centeredness? How does the Good Shepherd show His selflessness?

3. What pressures from without and within tempt you to selfishness? What spiritual resources do you have to enable you to be a selfless leader?

4. If you didn't have biblical insights, what would be the limits of what you could know about people? What more can you know about them through the wisdom of the Bible?

5. What leader in the past has cared for you in a one-on-one relationship? What made that more effective than a group setting?

6. How can leaders use the difficulty and complexity of their task as an excuse for not shepherding the people they lead?

7. How have you seen leaders get diverted from their primary tasks by appealing side issues?

8. What interesting diversions try to pull your attention away from your primary responsibilities for people?

9. Give an example of a leader who ignored the personal needs of those he or she led. Next, give an example of a leader who cared for the personal needs of those he or she led. Describe the relative effectiveness of these leaders.

10. What skills would you need to work on to become a more caring leader?

Prayer Focus

- Read the shepherding prayer of Hebrews 13:20-21. Notice the requests of verses 18-19 that show a willingness to be cared for as well as to care.

- Pray for discernment to know the needs of those you lead and for determination to try to meet those needs.

- Ask God to strengthen the shepherding skills of those who care for you.

Optional Activities

1. Make a list of the people who are directly responsible to you as their leader. Leave a few lines between each name. Go back and jot down in the space you left the personal needs that you need to take into account or help to meet through your leadership.

2. Locate the word shepherd in an exhaustive concordance and look up every reference in your Bible. There are about 40 passages. Select the ones describing human leaders of God's people, and make a list of leadership principles from them.

Assignment

1. Each day this week, intentionally perform a caring act for a different person you lead.

2. Read chapter 7 of *Be a Motivational Leader* and preview the Group Discussion Questions.

3. Read 1 Thessalonians 1:7-2:10. How did the two-way communication between Paul and the Thessalonians assist the growth of the church?

Seven

Be a Communicating Leader

Session Topic

Effective leaders communicate continually about the goals and programs of their organization.

Community Builder (Choose One)

1. Describe a situation in which you told something to someone and then that information passed among several people until you heard it again in a distorted form.

2. Tell about a childhood experience when one or both of your parents didn't tell you about something important that was happening around you. How did you feel when you found out?

Group Discovery Questions

1. How do you think keeping people informed motivates them to feel a part of the group and to excel in their work?

2. When have you seen poor communication within an group tear down morale and worker effectiveness? When have you seen good communication build up morale and worker effectiveness?

3. Why do you think that some unwise leaders choose to withhold information from the people they lead?

4. Eims advises, "It is especially important for a leader to brief the people at the beginning of any project" (p. 72). Do you agree? Why or why not?

5. How have you seen good or bad communication at the beginning of a project effect the outcome of that project?

6. Read Proverbs 15:23. How do you think a leader can judge the right time for communicating information?

7. Read Proverbs 20:28. What do you think are some common leadership temptations to distort or slant information? Why should leaders resist those temptations?

8. Not everyone in a group should know everything. How can a leader determine what information is appropriate to share with which people?

9. How have you seen someone harmed by learning something he or she was not mature enough to handle?

10. Read Proverbs 16:23. How do people discern that leaders are sharing from their hearts and not just their heads when they communicate about the group?

11. How would you like to improve as a communicating leader?

12. How can you encourage those who lead you to communicate more effectively with you and others they lead?

Prayer Focus

- Read Paul's prayer about the basis of enriched speech in 1 Corinthians 1:4-9.

- Ask God for the wisdom required by leaders to communicate timely, accurate, appropriate, and motivating information.

- Pray for wise and honest communication at work, at church, and within local and national government.

Optional Activity

- Memorize the verses Eims used to identify the kind of information leaders should share: Proverbs 15:23 (timely information), Proverbs 20:28 (accurate information), Proverbs 15:2 (appropriate information), and Proverbs 16:23 (motivating information).

Assignment

1. Read Romans 16:17-27. List all the avenues of communication to the Romans that Paul mentioned. Then list the principles of communication you can derive from these verses.

2. Read chapter 8 of *Be a Motivational Leader* and preview the Group Discussion Questions.

3. Read 1 Timothy 1:3-7 as an example of both pointless and goal-oriented ministry.

Eight

Be a Goal-Oriented Leader

Session Topic

Effective leaders help those they lead establish both long-range and short-range goals.

Community Builder (Choose One)

1. When you were a child, what were some goals your parents set for you? What's the first goal you can remember setting for yourself?

2. What goal that you set and achieved are you most proud of? Why?

Group Discovery Questions

1. Why do you think people need goals in their lives and in their work?

2. Why do you think goal setting seems unspiritual to some people?

3. Give some examples of people in the Bible who set goals and worked toward them. Did God approve of what they did?

4. What are some differences between long-range and short-range goals?

5. What do you think happens to people or groups that set up short-range goals without a clear understanding of their long-range goals?

6. What are some of the goal-setting mistakes people make that can leave them frustrated and discouraged?

7. Solomon wrote, "A longing fulfilled is sweet to the soul" (Prov. 13:19). What does that proverb have to say about the relationship between goal setting and group morale?

8. How have you seen personal or group goals protect someone from getting off track?

9. What are the greatest benefits that you have seen come from good goal setting?

10. How can you become more aware of the goals of your church and get involved in reaching them?

11. What areas of your life or work would benefit most from some serious goal setting? What would you need to do to establish workable goals for those areas?

12. Imagine you have just established long-range and short-range goals. What help would you want from your leaders in implementing those plans?

Prayer Focus

- Read Romans 1:8-17 and 15:18-33 in which Paul prays about and discusses his long-range and short-range goals.

- Spend time in prayer and in reflection about the goals God wants in your life and area of leadership.

- Pray for wisdom in knowing how to institute new or revised goals for your life or work.

Optional Activities

1. Devise one long-range goal and two to four short-range goals for each of these areas of life: spiritual maturity, physical well-being, family life, and professional responsibilities.

2. Analyze Romans 1:8-17 and 15:18-33 and make a list of Paul's long-range and short-range goals revealed in these passages. Romans 15:16 states Paul's overall ministry goal. Arrange the other goals in order of importance under this one.

Assignment

1. Memorize Proverbs 16:3 as a scriptural encouragement to goal setting.

2. Read chapter 9 of *Be a Motivational Leader* and preview the Group Discussion Questions.

3. Read Nehemiah 5 and notice Nehemiah's decisive leadership in addressing the problem of exploitation of the poor by the wealthy.

Nine

Be a Decisive Leader

Session Topic

Effective leaders know how to make difficult decisions in a timely fashion.

Community Builder (Choose One)

1. Who's the most decisive person you know? What do you admire most about him or her?

2. When you were growing up, who in your family or neighborhood was known for making bad decisions? What were the results of those bad decisions?

Group Discovery Questions

1. What does Eims mean by the saying "The ministry is going great, but these decisions are killing me" (p. 90)? When have you felt that way?

2. How might personal insecurity contribute to difficulty in making decisions?

3. How might pride or laziness contribute to difficulty in making decisions?

4. What factors make decisiveness difficult for you?

5. How can a leader gain a clear definition of a group problem that requires a decision?

6. What do you think happens when leaders make decisions without a clear definition of the problem? Can you illustrate?

7. What does a leader gain by asking for suggestions from people before making decisions?

8. When there are several options to choose from in decision

making, how can you narrow the range of choices?

9. What role does your time alone with God play in your ability to make good decisions?

10. Preparation for good decisions is a group effort. How is implementing decisions a group effort too?

11. What kinds of decisions do you find easier to make? Which kinds do you find more difficult to make?

12. Is it easy or hard for you to ask for input from others when you have decisions to make? How can you strengthen your interaction with others in decision making?

13. What is the best decision-making process you ever observed or participated in? What factors made it outstanding?

14. Imagine you made a bad decision in leading a group. What do you think is the best way to handle it with the group?

Prayer Focus

- Read the decisive encounter of Jesus with the Devil in Matthew 4:1-11. Notice how clearly Jesus perceived the issues before responding and how important the mind of God was in each situation.

- Admit to God the deficiencies you sense as a decision-maker. Ask Him to grant you the courage, wisdom, openness, and confidence necessary to make tough decisions.

- Pray about decisions facing you and the groups you are involved with.

Optional Activity

- Interview a successful decision-maker about how he or she reaches high-quality decisions. Find out how this person clarifies problems, narrows options, makes the final choice, and implements the decision.

Assignment

1. Go through the eight steps of good decision making outlined in chapter 9 to deal with a personal problem this week. Make a written record of the results of each step.

2. Read chapter 10 in *Be a Motivational Leader* and preview the Group Discussion Questions.

3. Meditate on how Solomon's prayer in 1 Kings 3:5-10 applies to your needs for competence in your leadership responsibilities.

Ten

Be a Competent Leader

Session Topic

Effective leaders focus on excelling in the areas of ability God gives them.

Community Builder (Choose One)

1. What is an area of competence that you have that is just for fun—a hobby, sport, or special interest? How did you develop it?

2. Tell about a time when you had to deal with an incompetent person who couldn't do anything right. What was the outcome?

Group Discovery Questions

1. How do incompetent people ever make it into leadership positions? What kinds of things do organizations sometimes mistake for competency?

2. How have you sensed the competency of the good leaders you have worked with? How have you picked up on the incompetency of the worst leaders you have known?

3. Eims stresses that competent leaders know how to do the jobs God wants them to do. How can envy, pride, and guilt distract them from behaving competently?

4. How can you keep focused on your area of competency so you don't overstep into someone else's field of responsibility?

5. A good salesman may not make a good sales department head, for example. To be competent, what kinds of things do leaders need to know beside the mechanics of their business?

6. What are some ways competent leaders can increase their expertise? How do you try to increase your expertise as a leader?

7. What risks do otherwise competent leaders face if they cannot admit they need help in doing their jobs?

8. How can competent leaders give people confidence that they too can complete their jobs successfully?

9. What do you think is the relationship between learning leadership principles from the Bible and from other sources, such as classes, seminars, and books?

10. What do you think would make you a more competent leader in the areas of responsibilities you have? How could you acquire the training or skills you need?

Prayer Focus

- Read Paul's prayer for power for competency in Ephesians 3:14-21.

- Pray for insight and wisdom to understand those responsibilities and tasks that you need to know how to handle well in order to be a competent leader.

- Pray for the spiritual wisdom to resist the temptations of envy, pride, and guilt that can distract you from commitment to the tasks God has laid out for you alone.

Optional Activities

1. On a sheet of paper draw a rectangle that takes up about half the page and label it "My Field of Competency." Inside the rectangle, list the responsibilities that you need to master. Outside the rectangle, list the responsibilities that belong to others in your group. Highlight the items inside the rectangle that you need to pay more attention to.

2. Memorize the following verses about competent leadership: Proverbs 10:14; 1 Corinthians 4:7; 2 Corinthians 10:12-13.

Assignment

1. Write a note of appreciation to a leader whose competence you admire. Commend that leader for at least one of the traits of competency identified in chapter 10.

2. Read chapter 11 of *Be a Motivational Leader* and preview the Group Discussion Questions.

3. Read Jesus' prayer for unity on the part of His disciples in John 17:20-26.

Eleven

Be a Unifying Leader

Session Topic

Effective leaders foster group unity as evidence of group maturity and as a means to success.

Community Builder (Choose One)

1. What was a group activity you enjoyed when you were young? Who in that group was the unifier who pulled everyone together? How did that person unite all of you?

2. In your extended family, who is the member who draws people together and helps them get along? How does he or she do that?

Group Discovery Questions

1. Read Ecclesiastes 4:9-10. What practical truths does this passage express about the benefits of unity for any group?

2. Read Romans 15:5-6. What are the spiritual values associated with unity among Christian workers?

3. How have you seen these destructive agents tear down the unity of a group: Slander? Anger? Pride? Envy?

4. Read Proverbs 10:12. How should love "cover over all wrongs" within your group?

5. Read Proverbs 11:13 and 17:9 and Psalm 141:3. How do you think this sort of verbal protection can be developed in your group?

6. Read Proverbs 12:18 and 15:4. What can you do to encourage kind speech within your group? What natural tendencies would you have to overcome to speak positively about all of your coworkers?

7. Restraint on the part of a leader helps build unity. How well do you handle your temper when situations become heated? How can you improve your restraint?

8. Do you tend to project good humor or gloom to those you lead? How can you improve the unifying effect of your good humor?

9. Eims advocates friendliness between leaders and followers as a unifying factor (p. 115). Do you agree with him or favor emotional distance between leaders and followers? Why?

10. Apart from the practical benefits derived from unity, what theological reasons can you suggest for wanting unity within a Christian organization?

Prayer Focus

- Read the blessing of God that unites His people recorded in Numbers 6:24-26.

- Pray for the emotional and spiritual maturity to pursue unity in spite of all the frustrations of group life.

- Ask God to create a desire for unity and mutual concern within your workplace, church, and family.

Optional Activities

1. Identify a problem that your group needs to solve. Give the problem to a few individual leaders to work on alone for a few days. Then assemble the leaders to work on solving the problem together. Discuss with the group the benefits of united effort.

2. Identify the single greatest enemy of unity in your group. List four things you could do to combat that enemy. Rank them in order of importance. Begin to implement the best response.

Assignment

1. Pray every day this week for the unity in your church among the pastoral staff, the rest of the leadership, and the congregation.

2. Read chapter 12 of *Be a Motivational Leader* and preview the Group Discussion Questions.

3. From Ephesians 4:11-16 compile a description of the work leaders should do.

Twelve

Be a Working Leader

Session Topic

Effective leaders equip the next generation of leaders by example as well as by instruction.

Community Builder (Choose One)

1. Who was the best teacher you ever had? What made him or her so important to you?

2. Who has been the most important mentor in your Christian life? How did he or she influence you toward spiritual maturity?

Group Discovery Question

1. A mentor is a mature leader who tutors a younger leader. What qualities would you want in a mentor?

2. Who was your greatest mentor? What did you learn about being a mentor from that relationship?

3. Eims says a mentor needs to be a laborer who also trains others to labor. How would this idea apply to a pastor? A factory foreman? A parent? A corporate executive?

4. What do you think would be the greatest difficulties and frustrations in mentoring leaders?

5. How do you think a leader committed to mentoring the next generation of leaders can find the resources to persevere through the difficulties of the job?

6. What do you think would be the most significant rewards for engaging in mentoring future leaders?

7. What skills do you think you are equipped to pass on to others through a mentoring relationship?

8. What skills would you still like to learn through a mentoring relationship with a maturer leader?

9. In Christian ministry, when do you think a leader becomes too removed from the work of the group to engage in effective training of future leaders?

10. How do you think leaders who feel detached from the work of their groups can re-involve themselves and become effective mentors?

11. Read Ephesians 4:11-12. How are the leaders described in this passage both laborers and trainers?

12. How could the leaders in your church be freed to do more mentoring of leaders?

Prayer Focus

- Read Paul's prayer and admonition as Timothy's mentor in 2 Timothy 1:3-14.

- Give thanks to God for those who have been your mentors in your faith and in your work.

- Ask God's blessing on those whom you are leading that they will be effective coworkers and future leaders.

- Pray for wisdom in integrating into your life and leadership all of the many ideas God has impressed on you through the course of this study.

Optional Activities

1. Identify a leader in your group whom you would like to mentor. Explain to him or her what the goals, methods, and duration of this relationship would be. Refer periodically to *Be a Motivational Leader* as a way of staying on track as a mentor.

2. As further preparation for effective leadership, read *Be the Leader You Were Meant to Be* (Victor), also by LeRoy Eims.

Assignment

1. Make a list of people you have discipled formally or informally. Pray for them every day this week.

2. Make a list of people who have discipled you formally or informally. Pray for them every day this week.

3. Make a list of the most important leadership concepts you learned during the course of this study. Rank them in the order in which you need to put them into practice.